Making a Holy Lent

FR. WILLIAM CASEY, C.P.M.

Making a
HOLY
LENT

40 Meditations to Prepare You for
the Church's Holiest Season

EWTN PUBLISHING, INC.
Irondale, Alabama

Nihil Obstat: Very Reverend Bryan W. Jerabek, J.C.L., *Censor Librorum*
Imprimatur: + Robert J. Baker, S.T.D., Bishop of Birmingham in Alabama
December 3, 2017
Cum permissu superiorum.

EWTN Publishing, Inc.
5817 Old Leeds Road, Irondale, AL 35210

Distributed by Sophia Institute Press, Box 5284, Manchester, NH 03108.

Library of Congress Cataloging-in-Publication Data

Names: Casey, William (Priest of the Congregation of the Fathers of Mercy), author.
Title: Making a holy Lent : 40 meditations to prepare you for the church's holiest season / Fr. William Casey, C.P.M.
Description: Irondale, Alabama : EWTN Publishing, Inc., 2018.
Identifiers: LCCN 2017050817 | ISBN 9781682780503 (pbk. : alk. paper)
Subjects: LCSH: Lent—Meditations. | Catholic Church—Doctrines.
Classification: LCC BX2170.L4 C368 2018 | DDC 242/.34—dc23 LC
record available at https://lccn.loc.gov/2017050817

Behold, now is the acceptable time;
behold, now is the day of salvation.

—2 Corinthians 6:2

Contents

Making a Holy Lent

Introduction

This book is based on Lenten retreats I gave years ago to viewers of the Eternal Word Television Network. Its structure is suited both to television and to Lenten spiritual reading: seven chapters on seven topics to spread out over the forty days of Lent.

In the northern hemisphere, Lent occurs during the transition from winter to spring. This seems to me to be appropriate. Of course, spring brings with it themes of renewal and rebirth that are central to the Easter story. But the forty days leading up to Easter are also appropriate to the liturgical season: dark and slow, with the promise of beauty and light on the horizon approaching much more slowly than we'd like.

Making a Holy Lent

Now, my readers in Florida and California may not ordinarily experience the extreme variations in weather and temperatures that usually mark this change of seasons, but I live in Kentucky and travel extensively during Lent to conduct retreats such as this one. I've seen warm, mild winters and very severe, harsh springs. And I think, even in places with typically beautiful year-round weather, most people find that time seems to pass more slowly after the energy, anticipation, and activity of the Christmas season has passed. Students feel as though their studies are more tedious in the winter months than during the fall semester. Most of us feel a sense of the mundanity of the passage of time during this season of the year.

Because nothing is outside the providence of God, let me suggest to you that all this is by design. Lent was made for contemplation. It's a time when we are called to repentance, of course, but repentance requires reflection. We need to spend time thinking and praying about the most important truths of our Faith in order to discern where and how we can do better. This season — and this book — are meant to help facilitate that contemplation.

Here we will explore seven topics together: prayer, the true nature of the Church, the Real Presence in the Eucharist, the sacrament of Confession, the virtues of charity and chastity, the challenge of pride, and the queenship of the Blessed Virgin Mary. But there are also themes that run throughout that consistently remind us of the specialness of this season — confronting sin, honest self-reflection, repentance, and, most of all, the necessity of God's grace.

The reality and the experience of God's saving grace is really where everything comes together in this book and in the season of Lent. In prayer, we strengthen our relationship with God, humbly submitting our concerns, our challenges, and our gratitude to Him while He shares some of His life with us. In the Church, we see the medium through which sacramental grace comes into our lives and the visible sign of Jesus' covenant with us.

In the Real Presence our sharing of God's life goes to a new level, when, in His graciousness, God makes Himself fully present to us in the Blessed Sacrament. In the sacrament of Confession, we come to God so that He can graciously heal us through the Holy Spirit. In the virtues, we grow in grace *through* grace, allowing God to guide our growth in holiness. In humility, we empty ourselves, allowing God's grace to flow into and through us. And, finally, in the Blessed Mother we see the perfection that grace can achieve and a uniquely powerful and beautiful vessel through which that grace comes into our world and our hearts.

Making a Holy Lent

I hope and pray that these slow Lenten days will be grace-filled for you, and that this book will serve to highlight particular ways in which that grace can impact your life. These reflections should be simply a starting point for you to explore more deeply in prayer. Consider the specific ways these topics impact your life, and go to Jesus for help in developing and putting into action good resolutions that will endure beyond these forty days.

May God bless you on this Lenten journey.

Chapter 1

Prayer

During Lent the Church calls on us in a special way to prepare our hearts and to purify our souls so that we can be ready to commemorate the most important events in all of human history: the Passion, death, and Resurrection of Our Lord and Savior Jesus Christ. Our eternal destiny—whether we spend eternity with God or without Him, in happiness or in misery, in Heaven or in Hell—depends on how we respond to those events!

I have compiled this book—this written retreat—with one purpose in mind: to challenge you to answer the call that God has given to each and every one of you to be men and women of faith, prayer, and devotion. Let us use this season of Lent to get closer to God, maybe closer than ever before, so that you can be what God created you to

Making a Holy Lent

be: living signs, living witnesses, living instruments of His infinite love to the world.

For all of us, this should be a grace-filled time for personal repentance, spiritual renewal, and revival. It is a time when there should be one thing at the forefront of our minds — the salvation of our immortal souls. We must ask ourselves: Do I really believe that only God can totally satisfy the desires of my heart? It is, has been, and forever will be the case that only God can give us the kind of true peace and joy and happiness that we are searching for. Material goods cannot do that. Money cannot do that. Human relationships cannot do that. Only God can do it! God wants us to experience His infinite love and mercy and to respond to Him in a spirit of Christian joy.

How many of us can say honestly that we love God with all our heart and soul and mind and strength? Don't you know that is exactly the way God loves each and every one of us? It is not enough just to say that God loves us. It is better to say that God is infinitely *in love* with each and every one of us. And that is the way that God expects us to respond to His love.

We live in a time of great uncertainty. In fact, a great deal of the instability we see in the news and in our own communities finds its source in the *moral* and *spiritual* confusion of our culture. Our civilization needs a spiritual revival.

This spiritual renewal, however, cannot be imposed from above: It has to begin *with us*. It has to begin in our humble and contrite hearts because the world is never going to change unless there is first a change in the human heart. The world is never going to change for the better unless we are good. More precisely, the world is never going to be good unless we are holy. That was the central message of the Second Vatican Council more than five decades ago, and it's a lesson that has been lost by many Catholics today.

What is the best way to begin this process of individual spiritual renewal? If you haven't done so already in the season of Lent, the best way to begin is by making a good examination of conscience and a good Confession. The state of grace, to which we are restored by the grace of the sacrament, is the starting point for any personal renewal — and therefore is the starting point for the renewal of the world.

We find the image of all-consuming fire throughout Scripture. Sometimes this fire represents God's wrath and the just punishments He metes out, but just as often it represents the infinite love of God. God is Love. God is an All-Consuming Fire. Jesus said, "I came to cast fire upon

Making a Holy Lent

the earth; and would that it were already kindled!" (Luke 12:49). That fire is the fire of divine love, which should be burning in our hearts. It's the flame of the Holy Spirit. But like any flame, it must be kindled and then constantly rekindled, because otherwise it will eventually burn out and grow cold. The only way we can keep that fire of divine love burning in our hearts is through the power of prayer. So let us begin this mission at the beginning of our personal relationship with God by talking about the power of prayer.

There's no way any of us can reach our full spiritual potential as Christian men and women without a strong, deep life of daily personal prayer. True love demands union. True union with God comes only through the life of prayer.

I would be willing to bet that most Catholics could sum up their daily prayer life in half a minute or less. You might be one of them, and there would be nothing unusual about that. You might say a short prayer or two when you get up in the morning, then Grace before meals, then a few short prayers before bedtime. In the spirit of challenging you during this Lenten season, let me tell you: That is not good enough in the sight of Almighty God! God's love is constantly searching and thirsting and craving for more and more of our love in return! He is not going to fully satisfy your spiritual needs, and you are not going to be entirely pleasing to Him, unless you make the time and the effort to have a strong, deep life of daily personal prayer.

God told the prophet Jeremiah something that He intends for all of us to hear, understand, and never forget: "Before I formed you in the womb I knew you" (Jer. 1:5). Think about that for a moment. Our coming into this world was not an accident but an act of the Will of God. God in His infinite knowledge and wisdom has known each and every one of us from before time began. God created us out of nothing because He wanted us to have life. He wanted us to know the joy of being because ultimately He wants all of us to share perfect eternal happiness with Him in His heavenly kingdom.

It was not by accident, but by the creative Will of God that each one of us came into this world at a certain time, in a certain place, in a certain way, and in a certain family. God did not bring us into this world to abandon us. We know this because in the Gospel He has revealed Himself to us. One of my favorite verses in the Bible is also in the book of the prophet Jeremiah:

> I know the plans I have for you, says the Lord, plans for welfare and not for evil, to give you a future and a hope. Then you will call upon me and come

and pray to me, and I will hear you. You will seek
me and find me; when you seek me with all your
heart, I will be found by you, says the Lord, and I
will restore your fortunes. (Jer. 29:11–14)

God has a plan for your life that is going to end in eternal
glory — if only you will cooperate with the graces He wants
to give you. The Apostle St. Paul said, "We know that in
everything God works for good with those who love him"
(Rom. 8:28). And who are the ones who love God? Four
times at the Last Supper Jesus said to the Apostles, "He
who has my commandments and keeps them, he it is who
loves me" (John 14:21).

But Jesus also said:

Not every one who says to me, "Lord, Lord," shall
enter the kingdom of heaven, but he who does the
will of my Father who is in heaven. (Matt. 7:21)

Why do you call me "Lord, Lord," and not do what
I tell you? (Luke 6:46)

For many are called, but few are chosen. (Matt.
22:14)

Enter by the narrow gate; for the gate is wide and
the way is easy, that leads to destruction, and those

who enter by it are many. For the gate is narrow and the way is hard, that leads to life, and those who find it are few. (Matt. 7:13–14)

The Lord is clear that, contrary to popular belief, it is not quite as easy to get into Heaven as we've often been led to believe. This points us to three very basic truths of the spiritual life. First, no one can be saved without conforming his or her life to God's Will. There is only one way to get to Heaven and that is by loving God, and the only way we can definitively demonstrate that we love God is through our obedience to His holy wisdom and Will. All of us are called to holiness of life. Jesus said, "You, therefore, must be perfect, as your heavenly Father is perfect" (Matt. 5:48). Holiness, which is that alignment of the human will with the Will of Almighty God, is not an option, but a command from Our Savior.

Second, it is impossible for any of us to do God's Will without the help of God's grace. Human nature is weak, having been wounded by Original Sin. "The spirit indeed is willing, but the flesh is weak" (Matt. 26:41). All of us feel the attractive power of sin in our lives in many ways. We cannot make it alone.

Third, God's grace comes to us first through the sacraments, but most often through the life of prayer. Therefore,

Making a Holy Lent

no one can be saved without prayer. Prayer is the key to salvation. The whole mystery of human salvation — your whole future, your whole relationship with God — depends entirely on how much and how well you are willing to pray. The saints became saints because they understood the incomparable power of prayer! They knew that prayer has the power to change our lives and the lives of others — and they proved it with their lives.

God is a loving Father, Who always wants to share the endless treasures of His grace with us and with the people we love. But the question is this: If prayer has this kind of power; if God uses prayer to direct the course of events in our lives; if prayer is absolutely essential to our well-being both now and for all eternity, then why do we pray so little? How is it that so many of us always seem to have time for everything but prayer? If we can sit for hours in front of the television watching a movie or a ball game and think nothing of it, how can it be that even five or ten minutes of personal prayer each day is too much of a burden? God gives us so much! Why do we give Him so little of ourselves in return?

It is a spiritual tragedy for a Christian to sit for hours upon hours a night in front of the tube, and then get up from the couch at the end of the evening with his mind full of all the noise and nonsense and intrigue and sex and violence—and then claim not to have time to pray. Let me tell you: If we Catholics would spend as much time in prayer as we spend in front of the television, we could convert this entire country. We could bring our civilization back to Christ.

There are many reasons prayer ends up being a low priority in our lives. Sometimes it's simply because we don't have enough faith. We don't really believe that God is going to hear and answer our prayers. We don't really believe that God is infinitely wise and infinitely in love with each and every one of us, and that He hears and answers our prayers in the way He knows is truly best for us.

Sometimes we fail to pray because we aren't willing to wait for God to give an answer, and we don't have the patience to persevere. In our society, people want and expect and demand instant gratification. We think life ought to be like a fast-food restaurant! We want what we want when we want it. We don't want to persevere in prayer like the widow in Jesus' parable who pestered the unjust judge until the judge ruled in her favor (Luke 18:1–8).

And then sometimes we don't pray because we are just too proud to admit we need God's help. We think we can make it alone, but we're always kidding ourselves. We often

Making a Holy Lent

hear that the American spirit is characterized by rugged individualism, fierce independence, and self-sufficiency—and in many ways those can be admirable traits. But when those ideas get carried over into one's relationship with God, nothing good can come of it. That kind of "individualism" cuts us off from Christ, and our relationship with Him wastes away. Jesus said, "I am the vine, you are the branches.... Apart from me you can do nothing. If a man does not abide in me, he is cast forth as a branch and withers" (John 15:5–6).

But I think that most of the time we neglect prayer because we think we are just too busy. We're too preoccupied with the cares of the world and the hectic pace of our lives, so we don't make the time or the effort to pray the way we should. We can always think of a million excuses not to pray. But let's take Our Lord's words in the Sermon on the Mount and turn them around. Think of them in the negative. "Don't ask and you won't receive. Don't seek and you won't find. Don't knock and it won't be opened to you" (see Matt. 7:7). The cost of neglecting prayer is much higher than the cost of putting off that housework or project or television show.

I think we do well to try to think of our relationship with the Lord from His point of view, as far as that's possible for a human being to do. Suppose you have a son who has grown up and moved away from home. As time goes on, you realize that he hardly ever calls, not even on birthdays and holidays. He has his own life now, and you don't seem to be part of it anymore. But you do hear from him when he wants something from you—when he needs money or is in some kind of trouble. He will happily turn to you in a time of decision or desperation. But other than that, you know you won't hear from him at all. What would that tell you as a parent? How would you feel? You would know that this son was only using you as a means to an end, as a way to serve his own interests. That's not how love works, or what love is. You would know that even if this son had warm feelings for you, there was no real love there. This is exactly what can happen in your relationship with Almighty God.

Archbishop Fulton Sheen used to say that most people look at prayer like a parachute. Think of the way a pilot looks on a parachute: He always keeps it with him, but he hopes he'll never have to use it. He'll use it in an emergency, of course, but other than that, he'll ignore it. That's the way most people look at prayer. Many people, tragically, turn to God only when they want something for themselves or when some crisis comes up in their lives. They pray only when they feel like it—and rarely do they feel like it. And once they get what they want and their troubles blow over,

Making a Holy Lent

they stop praying altogether, and God won't hear from them until the next time a problem arises.

God is not a parachute. He is not like roadside assistance, always waiting for your call and ready to leap into action. He is not obligated to make instant miracles for you. Indeed, He is under no obligation to hear or to answer the prayers of those who have made themselves strangers to Him.

This is why so many of us never seem to mature spiritually: When we actually make the time to pray, we do so selfishly. We pray with an eye on what we are going to get out of the transaction. We're not motivated by true love of God and neighbor. One of the most important of the spiritual works of mercy is to pray for your neighbor! It is not good enough just to pray for ourselves and the things we think are important to us. All of us have a serious obligation before God to pray for others, especially those most in need of our prayers — the sick, the suffering, those who are walking in darkness, and the innocent victims of war, violence, starvation, poverty, persecution, homelessness, and injustice, wherever they might be.

We are living in a world filled with suffering souls desperately in need of God's grace. Just log on to the Internet or scroll through social media, and you'll see how many lives and souls are hanging in the balance at every moment. How many could still be saved if only more people like us would pray in charity for them? Our Lady of Fatima said, "Pray, pray very much. Make sacrifices for sinners. Many souls go to hell, because no one is willing to help them with sacrifice."

This is why, when Jesus taught us to pray the Our Father, He did not tell us to say, "Give *me* this day *my* daily bread," but, "Give *us* this day *our* daily bread." It wasn't, "Forgive *me my* trespasses," but, "Forgive *us our* trespasses." And it wasn't, "Lead *me* not into temptation," but, "Lead *us* not into temptation." And that is because a mature faith — true Christian spirituality and charity — does not merely pray for itself. When we have that maturity, we pray for the needs of others, and we give God thanks and praise and adoration, and we make reparation for sin.

Prayer is essential for salvation, but that does not mean it will make our lives perfect in this world. It's easy to think that, once we begin to make time for daily prayer and practice the spiritual life in earnest, everything in our lives ought to go beautifully. But anyone who has read the lives of the saints knows how false that is. God invariably permitted the saints to be tried like gold in the fire of suffering, tribulation, and persecution; by these means He gave them the opportunity to practice heroic virtue. They

Making a Holy Lent

bore the heaviest crosses until the day, the hour, and often the moment they died. If you read the Bible from cover to cover, nowhere will you find God promising anyone perfect contentment and fulfillment here and now. He makes that promise to us only in the life to come — and then only for those who are faithful, who keep the Commandments, who pray.

Jesus said, "If any man would come after me, let him deny himself and take up his cross daily and follow me" (Luke 9:23). And we have to pray for the grace to bear that cross with patience and a spirit of self-sacrifice and Christian love. God will never permit a cross to come into our lives that is too heavy for us to bear. Further, when we offer our daily sufferings in the form of prayer — when we unite our daily crosses with the suffering of Christ on Calvary — our sufferings take on a tremendous redemptive value. These prayers obtain for us and for others many special graces. Therefore, when we offer our daily burdens to God, nothing that we suffer will ever be in vain. All of it is turned into a most powerful prayer.

God hears every prayer in His time and in His way, so when we pray, we are always going to get one of three responses from Him: "yes," "no," or "wait." Why does God not always give us everything we ask for in prayer? It is precisely because God is the most loving of fathers, Who is all knowing and all powerful; He sees the future with perfect clarity, including every possibility and every contingency, so He knows what is going to happen if we should get some of the things we ask for. He knows, that is, that we don't always ask for things that are truly good for our spiritual welfare.

If your little child were to ask you for a sharp knife to play with, would you give it to him? Or if he asked for a cigarette lighter or a pack of matches or a .38 special, would you give it to him? Of course you wouldn't! You can foresee that any of those things could hurt him or others, and so it is out of love that you refuse. No matter how much your child might cry out to you, you won't give him any of those things. It is the same with God. When we pray, we know God will give us nothing that will lead our hearts away from Him and His kingdom.

God may not always give us everything we want, but He will surely give us the things we truly need. Sometimes our wants and needs are the same, but sometimes they are not—and often only God knows the difference. We must trust that He can arrange things for our happiness far better than we can, and so we should pray with trust, confidence, humility, and perseverance.

The Gospel shows us that Our Lord was Himself an example of a life devoted to prayer. Jesus spent long days teaching, preaching, healing, and performing miracles—but whenever the opportunity arose, He would draw apart from everything and everyone to be alone with the Father in prayer. The Son of Man was not *too busy* to pray. When He wanted to pray, He would withdraw to a secluded place: to the top of a mountain or into the desert. Before every important action of His life, He drew apart to be alone with the Father in prayer, and He did this to leave us an example to follow. The best, simplest, and most effective way to pray is to be alone with God and to speak to Him from the heart.

Speaking to God from the heart is the essence of mental prayer; it is a conversation with God. St. Teresa of Avila defined mental prayer as intimate conversation with Him by Whom we know ourselves to be loved. Prayer must be more than just the mouthing of pious words! Prayer cannot be just a habit. It has to come from the heart. The best way to pray is to speak to God the way you would speak to the person whom you love the most in the world.

Our prayers have a very special power when we come before Our Lord in the Blessed Sacrament. This is the secret the saints knew: that there was practically no grace or favor, in keeping with God's Holy Will, that Our Lord would refuse to grant them when they came before Him in His Eucharistic Presence. The Mass is an immense, inexhaustible treasury of graces. Jesus Christ places Himself in the hands of the priest as a Victim — a Victim of infinite value — to obtain for us all the graces and all the blessings we need.

Without prayer, we will cut ourselves off from this treasury of God's grace. Without prayer, we will drift away from God and grow lukewarm. Without prayer, we will give in to temptation, fall into sin — maybe mortal sin — and fall away from the Faith. With prayer, we draw close to God and learn to know and to love Him. With prayer, God reveals Himself to us, speaks to our hearts, and guides our lives by the light of the Holy Spirit. With prayer, He makes all things work together for the good of those who love Him (Rom. 8:28).

It has been said many times that we bring nothing into this world and that we will take nothing out of it when we die. In a material sense, this is true. But in a spiritual sense, it is not, because the spiritual fruits of our faith, our prayers, and our good works are a treasure that we have stored up in Heaven. God will let us keep only as much as we are willing to give away in life — what we are willing to sacrifice for others and for Him, including our time spent in prayer. What a terrible thing it would be one day to have to stand before God empty-handed!

Making a Holy Lent

The Apostle St. James wrote, "What is your life? For you are a mist that appears for a little time and then vanishes," and we know how true that is (James 4:14). Life is short—too short, for all of us. We have come from God and we are going back to Him. Not a single one of us knows with any guarantee whether we're going to live to see even one more day on this earth. Every moment we are here is precious to us because every moment we really are making and shaping our eternal destiny.

So let's make the most of the gift of life and the gift of time that God has given us. The time to store up your treasure in Heaven is now. The time to be reconciled with God and with your neighbor is now. The time to give of yourself to others is now. The time to make a new commitment to Jesus Christ and His Church is now. If you haven't done it already, start today. This Lenten mission is the perfect occasion to make a new start. Please don't put it off until tomorrow or next week. Before you know it, life can and will pass you by.

Every day dedicate some time to conversing with God. This is sincere proof of your love for him for love always seeks to be near the beloved. This is why prayer should be put before everything else. Whoever does not understand this or does not put it into practice cannot excuse himself by saying he has no time; ... he has no love.[1]

The time to answer God's invitation to a deeper prayer life is now. If you do so, then one day, when you have left this world, you will have the joy of hearing Our Lord say to you, "Come, O blessed of my Father, inherit the kingdom prepared for you from the foundation of the world" (Matt. 25:34).

[1] St. John Paul II, Homily, April 7, 1987.

Chapter 2

The Catholic Church

Let's begin this chapter with a few questions:

- What is the one Church founded immediately, directly, and personally by Our Lord Jesus Christ when He was on earth?
- What is the only Church that has existed continuously for twenty centuries, from Pentecost to the present?
- What is the only international worldwide united body of Christian believers in the world, the only one united in faith, worship, and government?

The answer to all of these questions, of course, is the Catholic Church.

Making a Holy Lent

Here is how *Lumen Gentium*, the Second Vatican Council's Dogmatic Constitution on the Church, describes the Church and Her role in our lives and salvation:

> Lifted above the earth, Christ drew all things to Himself. Rising from the dead He sent His Life-giving Spirit upon the disciples and through the Spirit established His Body which is the Church as the Universal Sacrament of Salvation. Seated at the Right Hand of the Father, He works unceasingly in the world to draw all men into the Church and through it, to join them more closely to Himself, nourishing them with His own Body and Blood and so making them share in His life of glory. (no. 7)

Wherever I go, I find that more and more Catholics, especially young Catholics, don't seem to have any idea what it means to be Catholic — no idea what the Catholic Church is or what She's about or where She came from, and no idea what sets Her apart from other religious institutions. This has made younger Catholics, many of whom don't even know the basics of their Faith, easy prey both for fundamentalist sects who peddle simplistic and false interpretations of the Bible and for the secular, materialistic, pagan culture we live in. Millions of baptized Catholics have become totally caught up in the mad, mindless pursuit of the so-called American dream, the endless chase after success, status, comfort, pleasure, money, sex, power, and all those other things that have no value whatsoever in the sight of Almighty God.

During the First Gulf War, an American general described the American strategy against the Iraqi Army like this: "First we are going to cut it off, and then we are going to kill it." That is exactly the strategy Satan uses against our young people. First, he tries to cut them off from the Catholic Church, from the source of grace, from the Mass and from the Holy Eucharist, from the rest of the sacraments, especially the sacrament of Penance, and from the life of prayer. Then he tries to get them to live habitually in mortal sin. And once he has done that, he knows he can destroy them.

It is best to start at the beginning—with the Holy Scriptures. As Catholics, we have to know the Bible better than our Protestant friends do. And we have no excuse, because the Bible comes from the Catholic Church! The Bible—that collection of divinely inspired books that make up the Old and New Testaments—was put together by the Catholic Church. Out of thousands of early Christian and ancient Jewish writings, the Church had to decide

Making a Holy Lent

which were authentically the Word of God and which were not. The ones that were accepted were pronounced to be divinely inspired by the authority of the Church — the authority given to the Church by Jesus Christ through the Apostles and their successors.

There are two sources of God's revelation to humanity: the Bible, which is God's Written Word, and the Apostolic Tradition, those matters not written down but passed on through the Church, which is God's living voice. The Church, more precisely, is a living teaching authority established by Christ Himself to interpret Divine Revelation for us and to govern and sanctify the people of God. If you say the Bible is the sole rule of faith, you're going to be left with an insurmountable problem; you're going to have as many denominations as you have interpretations of the Bible! That is not what Our Lord established. And that is why the Bible itself says that *the Church* is "the pillar and the bulwark of the truth" (1 Tim. 3:15).

Now, Our Lord used the word "Church" in only two places in the Gospel. The first is when He posed this question to the Apostles:

> "Who do men say that the Son of man is?" And they said, "Some say John the Baptist, others say Elijah, and others Jeremiah or one of the prophets."

He said to them, "But who do you say that I am?" Simon Peter replied, "You are the Christ, the Son of the living God." And Jesus answered him, "Blessed are you, Simon Bar-Jona! For flesh and blood has not revealed this to you, but my Father who is in heaven. And I tell you, you are Peter, *and on this rock I will build my church*, and the powers of death shall not prevail against it. I will give you the keys of the kingdom of heaven, and whatever you bind on earth shall be bound in heaven, and whatever you loose on earth shall be loosed in heaven." (Matt. 16:13–19, emphasis added)

In the second instance, Jesus was again speaking to the Apostles:

If your brother sins against you, go and tell him his fault, between you and him alone. If he listens to you, you have gained your brother. But if he does not listen, take one or two others along with you, that every word may be confirmed by the evidence of two or three witnesses. If he refuses to listen to them, *tell it to the church*; and if he refuses to listen even to the church, let him be to you as a Gentile and a tax collector. Truly, I say to you, whatever you bind on earth shall be bound in heaven, and

Making a Holy Lent

whatever you loose on earth shall be loosed in heaven. (Matt.18:15–18, emphasis added)

Let's carefully consider Our Lord's words to St. Peter in the first passage: "On this rock I will build my church." Notice that Our Lord did not say, "On this rock I will build *your* Church" or "*you* will build *your* church" or "*you* will build My church." He said, "*I* will build My Church." The Gospel shows us clearly that Jesus Christ established a Church to be especially His own, a Church that He endowed with the fullness of divinely revealed Truth to the world, and to give us everything we need for our salvation, especially the seven sacraments.

The Church is not an invisible fellowship of like-minded believers. Rather, She is an Organism, a real, visible, living Body with living members who are incorporated into Her by Baptism. And the Church has been given very real authority — apostolic authority — the focal point of which is the successor of St. Peter, the Pope.

There can be no doubt that during the twentieth century the Church was abundantly blessed by a series of undeniably holy popes. One of the most interesting popes in this era, Pius XII, has become controversial due to anti-Catholic historical revisionism. Pius XII was Bishop of Rome from the late 1930s through the 1950s, which was one of the most tumultuous periods in the Church's history. With the rise of Nazism and Communism, a world war, and nuclear weapons, everywhere it seemed there was violence, madness, and confusion.

Pius XII was faced with an overwhelming burden. Both he and his predecessor condemned Nazism, a position that resulted in his becoming a virtual prisoner inside the Vatican after German forces occupied Rome. During the war years, Pius XII personally approved and helped to organize an underground network of Catholic churches, houses, and monasteries that helped to hide Jewish people and other high-risk individuals from the Gestapo. Israel Zolli, the Chief Rabbi of the city of Rome during the war, credited Pope Pius XII with saving several hundred thousand Jewish people from the death camps. After the war, Pius XII received an official award in the newly formed state of Israel for his work on behalf of the Jewish people. The rabbi was so moved by the Holy Father's example that he converted to Catholicism as the war drew to a close.

During these years of upheaval, Pius XII had in his quarters at the Vatican a painting on which he meditated every day. It was a painting of the Apostles in a boat on the stormy lake with Jesus asleep in the back of the boat.

Making a Holy Lent

That picture reminded him of the frightening challenges the Church had faced for the past two thousand years. Whenever the Faith appeared to be in danger and it looked as if Our Lord was asleep, Jesus Christ would always rise to bring His Church through the storm. And He will always rise to rescue His covenant family, His covenant people, His Mystical Body, the Church.

Today, we know that the Church has seen better days than our own. We continue to witness the march of secularization: the collapse of moral principles, the decrease in religious practice, the retreat from the authority of the Church. But we must always remember that the Church has been through similar tribulations many times before. And no matter how bad things might seem to be in the Church and in the world today, and no matter how bad things might get, just remember this: You can read the end of the book—and we win! The Bible gives us the assurance of Christ's ultimate victory! In the end, the gates of Hell are not going to prevail against the Church founded by Jesus Christ.

History has proven time and time again that God always raises up the greatest saints in times of crisis and confusion in His Church. Think of St. Maximillian Kolbe sacrificing himself in Auschwitz. Think of St. Thomas More refusing to submit to the rogue king of England. Think of the innumerable saints and martyrs from the early days of the Church under Roman oppression. The present age will be no different, and we should thank God for this! We should thank God for giving us the opportunity to practice heroic virtue!

The scene from which Pius XII's favorite painting was taken is in the fourth chapter of St. Mark's Gospel. Jesus and the Apostles were on the stormy Sea of Galilee, and the Apostles feared that their little boat would capsize. They were afraid they were going to drown along with Jesus, Who was asleep in the back of the boat, and so they rushed to wake Him. And when they did so, He demonstrated His power over the forces of nature by commanding the winds and the waves to die down. Then He turned and scolded the Apostles for their lack of faith! He rebuked them for believing that He would abandon them in their time of danger.

When I read this Gospel, I can't help but think how much we can be like the Apostles. In the darkest hours of our lives, how ready are we to believe that Our Lord would abandon us? But it is precisely at those times that He is closest to us, ready to help us with His saving grace! This is one of the more important events in the Gospel, because it is meant to teach the Apostles, their successors, and all of God's people through every age that there will

Making a Holy Lent

be times in their lives and in the life of the Church when trouble will come.

In every life there will be times of crisis, hardship, personal tragedy, sickness, disappointment, sorrow, and failure; times when the cross will come into our lives and put our faith to the test. Those storms can and will arise without warning, and there's always the danger that they can overwhelm us unless we put all our faith and all our hope and all our trust in the One Who knows us and loves us and cares for us more than we do ourselves. "Cast all your anxieties on him, for he cares about you" (1 Pet. 5:7). "I can do all things in him who strengthens me" (Phil. 4:13).

Suffering is nothing new to the people of God. There have been many, many times in the history of the Church when God has called upon Catholics in great numbers to suffer and even to die for the Faith. In fact, more Catholics died in the persecutions of the twentieth century than at any time since Our Lord founded the Church, especially under the evil totalitarian regimes that proliferated throughout the century. But the Church endures through all the persecutions and all the wars and all the disasters, all the revolutions and all the upheavals and all the attempts to destroy Her.

The Catholic Church

The Catholic Church has withstood the test of time like no other institution in history. In the first three hundred years after Our Lord founded the Church, the Roman Empire — the most powerful empire the world has ever known — persecuted His followers, driving them underground into the catacombs. More early Christians were put to death than could ever be accurately counted. The first thirty popes were martyred or died in exile, including St. Peter. But even the might of the Roman legions could not stamp out the faith of those humble Christian believers — and the blood of the martyrs became the seed of the Catholic Faith.

Today, almost two thousand years later, Our Lord's promises remain unbroken. First, Jesus promised to be with His Church until the end of time. Before He ascended into Heaven, He said to the Apostles, "I am with you always, to the close of the age" (Matt. 28:20). Jesus personally founded His Church, giving His own divine authority to St. Peter and to the Apostles and promising that the gates of Hell would never prevail against it.

Jesus also promised that the Holy Spirit would lead and guide His apostolic Church in the fullness of truth until the end of time: "Heaven and earth will pass away, but my words will not pass away" (Matt. 24:35). And that is why through history, every attempt to destroy the

Making a Holy Lent

Church has always failed. The Church is something more than a human organization; She is a divine institution. She is the Mystical Body of Christ, established by God Himself in the Person of His Son, Jesus Christ! No man, no people, no army, no government can destroy the work of God.

This trust and confidence that we have in Jesus applies not only to the life of the Church but also to our own daily lives. So long as we are faithful, in everything we will have to endure in this life—all of our personal, financial, moral, and medical problems, all the loneliness, anxiety, stress, sorrow, and pain—we know that Jesus will always be there to help us when we turn to Him in prayer. And if ever it should seem as if Our Lord is abandoning us, we know that it simply is not true and it never can be true because He is the Light of the World, Who drives the darkness out of our lives. He is the Peace that will calm every storm in our hearts, just as He put an end to the storm on the lake.

The Catholic Church bears the four marks of the True Church that set Her apart from all the rest. She is one, holy, catholic, and apostolic.

The Catholic Church

The Church is *one* because She is a united body of believers under the leadership of a single visible head. Our Lord founded *one* Church. At the Last Supper, did He not pray that all would be one? Holy Scripture tells us that one of the fruits of the Holy Spirit's presence is unity, and so where the Spirit abides, there will be unity! That worldwide unity exists only in the Catholic Church.

The Church is Holy. The Church, of course, in her human dimension will never be *perfect* in the world. But She is now, always has been, and always will be *holy* because of the infinite holiness of her Divine Founder, Jesus Christ, the Son of God. She is holy *in spite of* the unholy lives and actions of so many of Her members who bring scandal upon Her. Our Lord chose Judas to be one of the Twelve Apostles to be for us an everlasting reminder and a warning that we would have to live with scandals in the Church.

The Church is Catholic. The word "catholic" was first used by St. Ignatius of Antioch, a disciple of the Apostle St. John, who was martyred in AD 107. He was the bishop of the first predominantly Christian city: Antioch in Syria. St. Ignatius used the term "catholic" to distinguish the true Church of Christ from the schismatic sects that had already risen in the first century. "Catholic" comes from the Greek word *katholicos*, which means "universal." The

Making a Holy Lent

Catholic Church unites us in the communion of saints. In his *Modern Catholic Dictionary*, the late Fr. John Hardon, S.J., defined the communion of saints as

> the unity and cooperation of the members of the Church on earth with those in heaven and in purgatory. They are united as being one Mystical Body of Christ. The faithful on earth are in communion with each other by professing the same faith, obeying the same authority, and assisting each other with their prayers and good works. They are in communion with the saints in heaven by honoring them as glorified members of the Church, invoking their prayers and aid, and striving to imitate their virtues. They are in communion with the souls in purgatory by helping them with their prayers and good works.[2]

The "catholicity" of the Catholic Church, therefore, extends into the supernatural realm, but it also extends across our world, bringing together men and women of every nation, race, and tongue. The Catholic Faith transcends every racial, ethnic, and cultural barrier.

[2] Fr. John Hardon, S.J., *The Modern Catholic Dictionary* (New York: Doubleday, 1980), 116.

The Catholic Church

The Church is Apostolic because our Pope and our bishops are true, historical successors of the Apostles, and thus their authority comes from Christ Himself. Jesus commissioned the Apostles: "Go therefore and make disciples of all nations, baptizing them in the name of the Father and of the Son and of the Holy Spirit, teaching them to observe all that I have commanded you" (Matt. 28:19–20). And the Apostles, before they died, ordained other men to take their places, men whom they called bishops. And those bishops ordained other bishops, who, in turn, ordained other bishops, and so on and so forth down through the centuries. And so the Catholic Church preserves a direct and unbroken line of succession that links Her bishops and priests with the twelve Apostles, and thus with Christ. That is where the authority of the Church comes from.

The Church is God's covenant family on earth; all of us are adopted sons and daughters of God through Jesus Christ by virtue of our Baptism. The Church is also the Mystical Body of Christ, the Living Body that carries on Christ's saving work in the world. We know that every living body must have a soul; a body without a soul is a corpse. The soul that gives life to the Mystical Body of Christ is the Holy Spirit. The Holy Spirit is the life principle of God's Church.

Making a Holy Lent

As I travel around the country preaching the gospel, it is always frustrating to see so much ignorance and indifference from so many people who call themselves Catholics. God told the prophet Hosea, "My people are destroyed for lack of knowledge." (Hos. 4:6). And St. Paul wrote to the Christians in Corinth, "For some have no knowledge of God. I say this to your shame" (1 Cor. 15:34). It cannot be that way with us! We have to know our faith and know it well. We have to be able to defend it, not just so we can evangelize, but even more importantly so we can hand it on to our young people.

Parents who take no interest in their children's religious education and spiritual formation are throwing them to the wolves in a godless world filled with spiritual dangers. Parents must know the Faith, because they can't give what they don't have.

Parents are always the primary teachers of their children in the Faith—through word *and* action. It's a responsibility that parents cannot in good conscience delegate to somebody else—not to their bishop, not to their pastor, not to their priests or deacons or to nuns or lay teachers or catechists. There's no substitute for good example and good teaching—that is, holiness—on the part of Catholic parents.

The Catholic Church

God sends Light into the world—both the physical light that dispels the darkness of the void and, in the wisdom and the prophecy and the *person* of Jesus Christ, the Light that dispels the darkness of sin. During the days of His public life, Our Lord founded a Church to continue to spread that Light and thus to be the means of our salvation—the vessel that carries us to Heaven. He endowed that Church with the fullness of divinely revealed truth and everything we need to be saved.

"No one comes to the Father, but by me" (John 14:6). The Church that makes this possible is the One, Holy, Apostolic Catholic Church.

Chapter 3

The Real Presence

If someone were to ask me what I think is the biggest single problem facing the Catholic Church today, I would answer without any hesitation that it is the widespread loss of faith in Our Lord's Real Presence in the Blessed Sacrament.

When you receive Holy Communion, the priest presents the sacred Host and says, "The Body of Christ," and you say, "Amen." That word "amen" is not just a ritualistic response but an affirmation of the truth of the priest's declaration. When you say "amen," you are acknowledging before God that you believe that what you are receiving is, in fact, of the Body and Blood of Christ hidden under the appearances of bread and wine. You are affirming that in the Holy Eucharist you receive Jesus Christ's Body, Blood, Soul, and Divinity.

Making a Holy Lent

The Holy Eucharist is the greatest of the seven sacraments because in it we are receiving not just the grace of Jesus Christ, but Jesus Christ *Himself*. The Eucharist is "the source and summit of Christian life."[3] As Archbishop Sheen was fond of saying, without Christ's Eucharistic Presence, the Catholic Church is just another Christian denomination among thousands. Without His Eucharistic Presence, our churches, in spite of their grandeur and beauty and the goodness of the people gathered in them, are mere buildings. They are meeting houses and prayer halls, but nothing more.

We must be able to make an extremely important theological distinction in regard to the ways in which God is present. Obviously, God is present everywhere; He is omnipresent. There is no place in the heavens or on the earth where God is not. But, in the Holy Eucharist, Jesus Christ, the Eternal Word made flesh, true God and true man, is uniquely present. He is not only spiritually present: He is also substantially present and bodily present. In the Most Blessed Sacrament, He is present in His divinity and His humanity! By the Will of God the Father, the sacred humanity of Christ is the greatest source of graces, blessings,

[3] Vatican Council II, Dogmatic Constitution on the Church *Lumen Gentium* (November 21, 1964), no. 11.

strength, divine assistance, and consolation given for our lives—for those who believe!

Let's turn now to the sixth chapter of the Gospel of St. John, where Our Lord first reveals His greatest gift to us —the gift of Himself in the Holy Eucharist. This is one of the most interesting and challenging parts of the entire New Testament, and also one of the most beautiful.

The chapter begins with the miracle of the loaves and the fish, when the Lord multiplied five loaves of bread and two fish to feed the hungry crowd of thousands who had followed Him. And then, later that day, while the Apostles were out in the boat on the lake, Jesus came to them, walking on the water. Our Lord showed them these two spectacular miracles on the same day precisely because He wanted to prepare them for the next day, when He would present them with something far more difficult to comprehend.

That next morning, in the synagogue in Capernaum, Jesus said this to His followers:

> I am the living bread that came down from heaven; whoever eats this bread will live forever; and the bread that I will give is my flesh for the life of the

Making a Holy Lent

> world.... Whoever eats my flesh and drinks my blood
> has eternal life, and I will raise him on the last day.
> For my flesh is true food, and my blood is true drink.
> (John 6:51, 54–55, NAB)

He repeated this message over and over again. Those in the synagogue heard Him clearly; there could be no doubt about His meaning. They knew what He was saying but it was just too much for them—too much even for some of His own disciples, who responded, "This is a hard saying; who can listen to it?" (John 6:60).

Why would Jesus say these things that were so incredible and so shocking? Why would He insist time and time again that they eat His Flesh and drink His Blood? To answer that question, and therefore to understand the Eucharist, we have to think back over three thousand years to the time of Moses and the Exodus, when God was preparing to free His chosen people from many years of cruel slavery in Egypt.

It was God's plan to free the Israelites and to punish the cruelty of the Egyptians with ten supernatural disasters. And after God had sent nine plagues, Egypt was close to collapse, but the pharaoh still refused to allow the Israelites to leave. So God sent the tenth plague, the most terrible of them all: the Angel of Death, whom Scripture calls "the

Destroyer," who would strike down the firstborn of every Egyptian family.

But before this happened, God commanded Moses to have every Israelite family take a spotless male lamb and slaughter it. They were to put the blood of the lamb on the wooden lintels of every Israelite home and the Angel of Death, seeing the lamb's blood, would pass over that house and spare the firstborn inside. But that wasn't all there was to God's command: Every Israelite family was also to prepare a sacrificial meal, a Passover meal. With unleavened bread and wine, they were to eat the lamb they had sacrificed. God commanded that every Israelite family—every man, woman, and child—eat the flesh of the lamb. They had to partake of the sacrifice physically.

If the Israelites had fulfilled God's command only partially—for instance, if they did not eat the flesh of the lamb—then at midnight they would have found their firstborn struck down with those of the Egyptians. They had to eat the flesh of the lamb; they had to partake of that sacrifice as a family, as a community, as a people. God's chosen people, therefore, were saved by the blood of the lamb *and* they were nourished by eating the flesh of the lamb as they began their march toward the Promised Land. The Passover lamb was therefore the sacrifice of the Old Covenant.

Making a Holy Lent

God chose the lamb to be this crucial sacrifice because the lamb has always been seen as the gentlest and most innocent of God's creatures. The blood of the lamb — the innocent one — had power to save the Israelites, however, only because it was *a foreshadowing* of an infinitely greater Sacrifice: the Sacrifice of the Redeemer, the Messiah, the Suffering Lamb of God, Who was still to come, the One Whose coming was foretold through the centuries by the great prophets.

Twelve centuries after the Exodus, St. John the Baptist, the last and the greatest of the prophets and the precursor of the Messiah, was baptizing people in the Jordan River when he saw Jesus coming toward him in the distance. The prophet called out, "Behold, the Lamb of God, who takes away the sin of the world!" (John 1:29). Jesus Christ is the True Passover Lamb, Who fulfills the Old Covenant and ratifies the New. He is the Lamb of God, Who opens the gates of Heaven by shedding His Precious Blood once and for all.

And then, three years after His baptism in the Jordan, at the end of His public ministry, when He celebrated that last Passover with the Apostles, Jesus Christ offered His life to the Father in sacrifice for our sins. Before He went to Calvary to shed His Blood on the wood of the Cross, He took unleavened bread and wine, just as the Jews had done for centuries—but this time *He* was the Sacrificial Lamb. He said, "This is my body which is given for you. Do this in remembrance of me" (Luke 22:19).

When Our Lord said those words, He instituted the priesthood of the New and Everlasting Covenant. By the sheer power of His word, Jesus Christ changed bread and wine into His Body and Blood and commanded the Apostles to do the same thing—the only thing He would ever command them to do in memory of Him. And down through the centuries God continues to command His faithful people—His New Covenant People—to eat the Flesh of the Lamb.

Christ's Eucharistic Body and Blood are the sacrificial meal by which God frees His new chosen people from a far more insidious form of slavery than even that imposed by the Egyptians—slavery to sin. The Old Testament Passover became the New Testament Eucharist, the sacrament of Christ's Body and Blood. The Mass, therefore, is the sacrifice of the New and Everlasting Covenant. That is why the Mass is the greatest act of worship the world has ever known or ever will know.

The Mass is the one, supreme, eternal act of worship of the Son of God. The Mass is the mystical renewal and re-presentation of Our Lord's sacrifice on Calvary. It is Calvary made present again, where the merits of His Passion

Making a Holy Lent

and death are applied to our lives. This means that all the graces and all the blessings and all the power that flow from His Sacrifice—His perfect obedience to the Father's Will, the shedding of His Precious Blood, His atrocious agony at Calvary—are all applied to our lives and for our needs, the needs of the entire Church, and the needs of the whole world.

That is the power of the Mass. The Mass is the miracle in which Jesus calls Christians of every age and every time and every nation to be present at the Last Supper and, in a mystical way, to come to Calvary to stand at the foot of the cross, to relive the hour of His Passion, and to be fed with the Bread from Heaven that becomes His Sacred Body by the power of God's Word—the same Divine Word that brought this world into creation out of nothing. We're saved by the Blood of the Lamb and nourished by eating the Flesh of the Lamb as we continue on our spiritual journey to the True Promised Land, which is God's Heavenly Kingdom. This is the Mystery of the Holy Eucharist, the center and the source of true Christian worship for all time.

In the last book of the Old Testament, God spoke to the prophet Malachi, to whom He foretold the end of the many sacrifices of the Old Covenant and the coming of the one, perfect sacrifice of the New Covenant: "From the rising of the sun even to the going down, my name is great among the Gentiles, and in every place there is sacrifice, and there is offered to my name a clean oblation: for my name is great among the Gentiles, saith the Lord of hosts" (Malachi 1:11, Douay-Rheims). That one eternal sacrifice is the Holy Sacrifice of the Mass. That is why, whether you know it or not, whether you understand it or not, whether you believe it or not, whether you take it for granted or not, and no matter where it is offered, no matter how poor the church, no matter how humble the congregation, no matter how ordinary the priest, the Mass is the greatest, the most powerful, the most awesome, the most sacred thing that takes place on the face of this earth! Nothing in this world can give God greater honor and glory and praise than the offering of the Mass. And that is why St. Padre Pio, the great mystic of the last century, used to say, "It would be easier for the world to exist without the sun than without the Mass."

At the synagogue at Capernaum, Jesus wished to prepare the Apostles and the rest of His disciples for the miracle of His Eucharistic Presence. Jesus said to them, "The words that I have spoken to you are spirit and life" (John 6:63). Remember what He had previously told them: "For my

Making a Holy Lent

flesh is true food, and my blood is true drink." The Greek word for "true" that the Apostle St. John uses in his Gospel is *alethos*, which means "real," "true," "actual," or "literal." There is absolutely no way that this Gospel term can be explained away or watered down. Our Lord said precisely what He meant: Real flesh! Real blood! Real food! Real drink!

But Jesus also said, "It is the spirit that gives life, while the flesh is of no avail" (John 6:63, NAB). There are many who claim that this statement lends itself to a merely symbolic interpretation (or even a negation) of Our Lord's emphatic insistence that His disciples eat His flesh and drink His blood. There are some who will even claim that Our Lord seemed to contradict Himself in this regard. This is impossible, of course: God cannot contradict Himself!

For Catholics, His meaning has always been abundantly clear: He intended for us to understand that His body is more than just flesh! His Sacred Body is no ordinary flesh, precisely because His Eucharistic Flesh is inseparably united to His divinity and to the Spirit of God! In saying that the words He has spoken are "spirit and life," He attempted to teach the disciples that what He was speaking of was a great supernatural mystery; the work of the Holy Spirit — something that could have no natural explanation. It was, in fact, something that could be accepted only with absolute faith and trust in His divine words.

The most interesting thing of all, though, is that Our Lord did not try to stop them. He let them go! Jesus did not say, "No! You misunderstood me! I was only using a figure of speech! It was all just a metaphor, just a play on words! I didn't really mean that you have to eat my Flesh and drink my Blood!" He said no such thing because they *heard* what He said and they *knew* what He said and they *understood* what He said, and they rejected it. Jesus Christ wasn't going to upend the truth to keep His followers around; He let them walk away because they refused to trust Him, because they did not have faith in Him.

The gift of faith is a very precious thing. It is God's free gift, one that can come only from Him through His Holy Spirit. There is nothing that we can do to merit that gift for ourselves. Indeed, faith is one of the most precious gifts that God can ever give because it is the beginning of our salvation. In the Letter to the Hebrews we read, "And without faith it is impossible to please [God]" (11:6).

One of the hardest things Our Lord will ever call upon us to believe in is His Real Substantial Presence in the Holy Eucharist, because we have to disregard the evidence presented by our senses and believe entirely in the Word of God. His Presence is hidden, veiled under the appearances

Making a Holy Lent

of bread and wine. We can see it only with the eyes of our minds, enlightened by the gift of faith, a gift that is given only to those who have the humility to open their hearts to the truth.

The Personification of Truth is Jesus Christ, Who is the Way and the Truth and the Life. There is no other. That is why, when Jesus asked the Apostles, "Will you also go away?" St. Peter spoke up for the other Apostles, as he so often did, and replied, "Lord, to whom shall we go? You have the words of eternal life" (John 6:67–68). Those words of eternal life demand that we believe in the Real Presence of Our Lord in the Most Holy Eucharist. That is what the Church has taught. That is what the whole company of the saints has testified to. That is what the people of God have believed and understood for two thousand years.

In the Bible we find the earliest account of the institution of the Holy Eucharist at the Last Supper in St. Paul's First Letter to the Corinthians:

> I speak as to sensible men; judge for yourselves what
> I say. The cup of blessing which we bless, is it not
> a participation in the blood of Christ? The bread

which we break, is it not a participation in the body
of Christ? (1 Cor. 10:15–16)

Later, St. Paul writes that what he received *from the Lord*
—not from any man—he has handed on to us.

For I received from the Lord what I also delivered to
you, that the Lord Jesus on the night when he was
betrayed took bread, and when he had given thanks,
he broke it, and said, "This is my body which is for
you. Do this in remembrance of me." In the same
way also the cup, after supper, saying, "This cup is
the new covenant in my blood. Do this, as often as
you drink it, in remembrance of me." For as often as
you eat this bread and drink the cup, you proclaim
the Lord's death until he comes.

Whoever, therefore, eats the bread or drinks
the cup of the Lord in an unworthy manner will
be guilty of profaning the body and blood of the
Lord. Let a man examine himself, and so eat of the
bread and drink of the cup. For any one who eats
and drinks without discerning the body eats and
drinks judgment upon himself. (1 Cor. 11:23–29)

What about the great saints who came after the Apostles? In those first centuries of the Church, what did the

Making a Holy Lent

most immediate successors of the Apostles teach and write about the Holy Eucharist? If you study the lives of the early saints and their writings, you will find that they were unanimous in their belief in and their understanding of the Real Presence. There can be no question about it: What they believe then is what we still believe today!

> I have no taste for corruptible food nor for the pleasures of this life. I desire the Bread of God which is the Flesh of Jesus Christ and for drink I desire His Blood. (St. Ignatius of Antioch, *Letter to the Romans*)

> No one may share the Eucharist with us unless he believes that what we teach is true.... We do not consume the Eucharist Bread and Wine as if it were ordinary food and drink, for we have been taught that as Jesus Christ Our Savior became a Man of Flesh and Blood by the power of the Word of God, so also the Food that our flesh and blood assimilates for its nourishment becomes the Flesh and Blood of the Incarnate Jesus by the power of His Words contained in the Prayer of Thanksgiving. (St. Justin Martyr, *First Apology*)

> When the chalice we mix and the bread we bake receive the Word of God, the Eucharistic elements

become the Body and Blood of Christ by which our bodies live and grow. (St. Irenaeus, *Against Heresies*)

Jesus took earth from earth, because Flesh is from the earth, and He took Flesh from the flesh of Mary. And because He walked here in this Flesh, He also gave us this Flesh to eat for our salvation. But no one eats this Flesh unless he has first adored it;... we would sin if we did not adore. (St. Augustine, *Commentary on Psalm 98*)

The bread and wine are not a type of the Body and Blood Christ! No one may say that! Rather, it is the very Deified Body of the Lord. He Himself said, "This is My Body," not a type of My Body and "This is My Blood," not a type of My Blood, My Blood! (St. John of Damascus, *Of the Orthodox Faith*)

Nothing could be more beneficial for the life of the soul than making a worthy Communion — and nothing could be more damaging than making an unworthy one. That is why no one should ever come forward to receive Holy Communion without true faith in the Real Presence. St. Paul said, "For any one who eats and drinks without discerning the body eats and drinks judgment upon himself"

Making a Holy Lent

(1 Cor. 11:29). This is also why no one should ever come forward to receive Holy Communion while conscious of being in a state of mortal sin; that is the sin of sacrilege. Therefore, the Mass must never become an empty ritual to you; it must never become simply part of your weekend routine or a habitual obligation to get out of the way!

The Mass is Spirit and Life. If we claim that we don't get anything out of it, it can only be because we don't put anything into it. I always pray that God would give every Christian the grace to be able to see the Mass for what He intended it to be — a personal encounter with the Living Jesus Christ. One of the great tragedies of our time is that, in so many of our churches and even seminaries, Jesus in the Blessed Sacrament is surrounded by so much indifference and ingratitude and even neglect. It is devastating to think of all the graces that are lost due to this nonchalance about Christ's Eucharistic Presence, and how so many souls are suffering because so many Catholics ignore His Real Presence every day of their lives.

I can't tell you how disappointing it is to see that, in so many of our churches, the faithful don't bother to genuflect or to make any gesture of reverence toward Our Lord in the tabernacle. It's as if they don't have any idea Who is present in the tabernacle, as if they have no idea about the truth of the Real Presence. When I see all the chitchat and laughing and carrying on before Mass—it's as if Our Lord were not even there.

When I see all this irreverence, I can't help but think: Is it any wonder we have a vocations crisis? Is it any wonder that so many of our seminaries are empty or shut down? Do we honestly believe that God is going to reward us by sending good and holy vocations to the priesthood and religious life when His Son is surrounded every day by sacrilegious disrespect in His own House? It's not going to happen unless *we* change, unless *we* restore reverence in our churches and to the worship of Our Lord in the Blessed Sacrament. We genuflect out of respect and awe and humility—and because the Word of God tells us so (and then some): "At the name of Jesus every knee should bow, in heaven and on earth and under the earth, and every tongue confess that Jesus Christ is Lord, to the glory of God the Father" (Philippians 2:10–11).

As Catholic men and women, we are supposed to be filled with the love of Christ, and what could be more natural than to want to be with the one you love? If you really love someone, you always want to be present to that person; when a man and a woman are truly in love with each other, they always want to be together. And here's the beautiful thing: Jesus is always present to us in the Blessed Sacrament. He is here, an extension of His glorified life

Making a Holy Lent

in Heaven. We have the Living Risen Lord Jesus Christ truly and substantially present. In His glorified state He is not subject to the limitations of space and time, so He can be and is present in all the tabernacles of the world.

Seven centuries before Christ, the prophet Isaiah foretold His coming: "Behold a virgin shall conceive, and bear a son, and his name shall be called Emmanuel" (Isa. 7:14, Douay-Rheims). "Emmanuel" means "God with us." The Holy Eucharist is God with us and among us; He is the Source of all graces. The Eucharist is Jesus Christ waiting for us to come to Him day and night, waiting to share the treasures of His grace with us and with the people we love.

When we come before Our Lord in the Blessed Sacrament and trust in the power of prayer, we draw strength from *His* inexhaustible strength. We draw power from *His* inexhaustible power. We draw peace from *His* inexhaustible peace. He is the one who makes all our prayers and all our efforts bear fruit. Many times throughout his pontificate, Pope St. John Paul II directed the faithful to make the Eucharist the source of our strength. And St. Maximillian Kolbe is said to have remarked that "if Angels could be jealous of men, they would be so for one reason: Holy Communion."

At the Last Supper, when Our Lord gave us the Holy Eucharist, He said to the Apostles, "Apart from me you can do nothing.... If you abide in me, and my words abide in you, ask whatever you will, and it shall be done for you" (John 15:5, 7). Without Him, we can do nothing. Without Him, we are nothing. But thanks be to God, *He is the one who makes something out of nothing.*

It has always been true to say that every one of us needs to have a personal relationship with Jesus Christ. It's a constant theme in Evangelical Protestantism: the need to accept Jesus Christ as our personal Lord and Savior. But whenever I hear that, my response is *to thank God that I'm a Catholic*, to thank God for the Apostolic Church, and to thank God for the Holy Eucharist because the summit of that personal relationship with Christ is when we are united with Him spiritually and physically in the Sacrament of His Body and Blood—in Holy Communion, where Jesus is present to us in His Body, Blood, Soul, and Divinity.

Remember this, and never forget it: It just can't get any more personal than that.

Chapter 4

The Sacrament of Confession

Lent is the time of year when God obligates us to prepare our hearts and to purify our souls so that we are ready to receive Our Lord in His glorious coming at Easter. There's no time to delay. The Bible says, "Behold, now is the acceptable time; behold, now is the day of salvation" (2 Cor. 6:2).

During this season, every day we should try to make a good examination of conscience by asking ourselves these questions:

- Is there something I can do to get closer to God?
- Is there something I can do to know God better and to love Him more?
- Is there some way I can increase my desire for prayer?

Making a Holy Lent

- Is there some way I can rekindle that fire of divine love that might have gone out in my life?
- Is there some way I can rid myself of the spiritual mediocrity, the spiritual indifference that I find myself in so much of the time?
- Is there something I can give up?
- Is there something in my life right now that is not pleasing to Almighty God?
- Is there some sin that I am holding on to?
- Is there some habitual sin that is separating my heart from God's loving grace?
- Is there something I need to confess?
- Am I crucifying Our Lord all over again by living in my sins?

Further, we should pray every day:

Lord, let there be less of me and more of You. Let me say no to my will and yes to Yours. God, give me the grace to love You more today than yesterday and more tomorrow than today.

The Fatima seer Jacinta spoke this challenging truth: "If men only knew what eternity is, how they would make all possible efforts to amend their lives." With this in mind, let us explore the special grace God gives us in the sacrament of Confession to help us on that journey of sanctification.

The Sacrament of Confession

Our Lord warned us throughout the Gospel to be watchful. We must be on our guard, and that means keeping our souls in the state of grace, because we can never know the day or the hour when He will come. This applies not just to Our Lord's Second Coming, but also to our own death. The end of the world for each of us is the moment we die—and it could come at any moment. Therefore, we must keep our souls in the state of grace.

To help us to do that, Almighty God has given us the great gift of His Mercy in the Sacrament of Penance. It has become painfully obvious to me, both from personal pastoral experience and from polling data, that the vast majority of Catholics in our country gave up the practice of sacramental Confession long ago. This is truly a tragedy. First of all, the sacrament of Penance is the ordinary means for the forgiveness of mortal sins committed after Baptism. But it is also a veritable treasure of graces and spiritual strength for us in our daily struggle against sin and temptation.

Pope Pius XII said many times that the great sin of our age is, in fact, the denial of sin. "Sin" has become a dirty word that we don't want to mention anymore, even from the pulpit. Doesn't it strike you as odd that the more sin

Making a Holy Lent

there is in the world, the less Catholics—clergy, theologians, and laypeople—seem to say about it? This is theological insanity. Worse, it is spiritual suicide. There is only *one thing* that can separate us from God, and that is mortal sin. To conceal the reality of sin is, quite simply, to play the devil's game. It is to fall into his trap.

We have witnessed the dangerous encroachment of modern popular psychology on Catholic theology, certainly in academic circles. The result has been that any discussion of sin—anything that might cause people to have feelings of guilt or apprehension—is seen as "bad psychology." We focus more on that which affirms us as we are than on that which points to where we should be. We obsess over how to feel good about ourselves, how to build up our self-esteem, how to achieve self-actualization, and how to find our ultimate happiness and fulfillment and contentment in a purely worldly sense, without reference to God.

I am reminded of the words of St. Paul: "For the time is coming when people will not endure sound teaching, but having itching ears they will accumulate for themselves teachers to suit their own likings" (2 Tim. 4:3). That day has now arrived. Most people today see enjoyment of this life as being more important than eternity. We don't want to hear the truth because the truth makes us feel uncomfortable — because the truth sometimes demands that we change our lives, our minds, and our hearts toward God and toward others.

We are so afraid of rubbing people the wrong way that we shy away from speaking the whole truth. We shy away from preaching the gospel in its fullness. We don't want to give people the disturbing news that mortal sin separates us from Heaven and that Hell is real. We withhold essential parts of God's truth from His people. We forget that Jesus said to His disciples, "Woe to you, when all men speak well of you, for so their fathers did to the false prophets" (Luke 6:26).

What would you think of a physician who cared nothing about disease — didn't want to talk about it, didn't want to treat it, didn't want to be bothered about it, didn't care a thing about the physical health of his patients? Suppose someone was suffering from a serious illness and made a visit to this doctor, and even though his symptoms were clear and dangerous, this doctor, out of some misguided fear of upsetting his patient, concealed from him the gravity of his illness: "Don't worry about it! There's nothing wrong with you! You're going to be fine. Come back and see me again next year." But a year from now the patient may well be dead.

A doctor like that would be guilty of gross professional negligence and sued for malpractice. So, what would you

Making a Holy Lent

call a priest — or, for that matter, a Catholic layperson in a position of authority among family and friends — who is afraid or doesn't care enough to speak out against sin? What would you call the physician of the soul who will not deal with the one thing that can kill the life of grace in the soul? The patient who dies of his illness because of a neglectful doctor would lose only his physical life, but when we fail to speak out again sin, others may well lose their immortal souls.

I find it incredible that those who care enough about souls to speak up courageously against sin will often be labeled old-fashioned, insensitive, divisive, and judgmental — while the ones who maintain a culpable silence, those who tell people only what they think they want to hear are seen as understanding, sympathetic, pastorally sensitive, and merciful. This is nonsense! God said to the prophet Ezekiel, "If I say to the wicked, 'You shall surely die,' and you give him no warning, nor speak to warn the wicked from his wicked way, in order to save his life, that wicked man shall die in his iniquity; but his blood I will require at your hand" (Ezek. 3:18). It is never mercy to affirm people in their sins or to remain silent in the face of wrongdoing. That is the most merciless thing that I can think of. And the greatest love of all is concern for your loved ones' eternal salvation.

The Sacrament of Confession

Everywhere we see a dramatic rise in dishonesty, corruption, practical atheism, materialism, greed, selfishness, drug abuse, alcohol abuse, child abuse, hatred, false religion, sexual immorality, and sins against the sanctity of human life. In our culture, grave sin is practiced and tolerated as if it were just another part of our way of life!

And yet, there are Catholic parishes all over this country where every Sunday at every Mass, everyone in church comes forward to receive Holy Communion and almost no one goes to Confession! Where this is the case, we know that something is very seriously wrong. To receive the Eucharist consciously in a state of mortal sin is *yet another* mortal sin: sacrilege. This state of affairs is a sign that people don't want to recognize the reality of sin in their lives. It is a sign that people may well be growing content and satisfied to live in their sins and gamble the salvation of their souls.

When Jesus called the twelve Apostles and began to send them out to preach, He gave them authority and the power to cure the sick and to raise the dead and to give sight to the blind, the power to cast out demons and to make cripples walk—the power, that is, to bring healing to every kind of human suffering. But the Gospel also tells us that,

Making a Holy Lent

despite that awesome authority, the most important mission that Christ gave the Apostles was to preach the need for repentance. "Repentance" is one of the most important and most frequently used words in all of Sacred Scripture.

Jesus' first words when He began His public ministry were, "Repent, for the kingdom of heaven is at hand" (Matt. 4:17). And Our Lord told the Apostles that, in any place where people refused to hear that word and act on it, they were to leave that place and to shake the dust from their feet as a testimony against those people (Matt. 10:14.) Every messenger ever sent by God in both the Old and New Testaments was sent to preach a message of repentance. No one can be a disciple of Christ, or even claim the name "Christian," unless that person is willing to repent.

What exactly are we talking about when we speak of repentance? First and most simply, to repent means to recognize the reality of personal sin in your life — and to turn away from it. It means putting sin out of your life and changing your life according to God's Will, even when God's Will doesn't conform to your opinions.

Secondly, to repent means to seek the loving mercy of God with a spirit of true contrition. Contrition is more than just sorrow for sin; there are three elements to true contrition: sorrow for the sins you've committed, hatred for those sins and all sin, and a firm purpose of amendment, which means that you intend to try, with the help of God's grace, not to commit the same sins in the future.

Third, to repent means to accept God's word and God's law and to make it your way of life. It means putting faith into action. We are saved by faith working through love. Salvation is not by faith alone, and it never was. The Apostle St. James wrote, "Faith by itself, if it has no works, is dead" (James 2:17). Our faith must be a living faith. It can't be inactive or moribund. That won't cut it with God.

And finally, to repent means to do penance. Whether we realize it or not, even our most hidden sins in some mysterious way disturb the entire order of God's creation. They cause a diminishing of grace in the Mystical Body of Christ. God expects us to make reparation for the harm caused by our sins against Him and against our neighbors.

None of us will ever see the vision of God in Heaven unless we are humble enough to know and to admit that we are sinners in need of God's mercy. There are no exceptions. We should never be ashamed or afraid to admit that because the Bible says that "all have sinned and fall short of the glory of God" (Rom. 3:23).

Even though Original Sin is taken away by Baptism, Jesus knew that we would have to live with the effects of

Making a Holy Lent

Original Sin all through our lives. Our poor human nature is weak, wounded by Original Sin, wounded by the loss of grace incurred by all humanity because of the sin of our first parents, Adam and Eve.

This is why there is something about us that's always so strongly inclined toward sin. Within every human soul there is a struggle between good and evil, light and darkness, virtue and vice. Jesus said to His Apostles in the Garden of Gethsemane, "The spirit indeed is willing, but the flesh is weak" (Matt. 26:41). All of us feel the attractive power of sin in our lives. All of us have to struggle to control our disordered passions. There's always the danger that we can give in to temptation and fall into mortal sin in a moment of weakness. Therefore, there's an ongoing need for repentance in our lives.

In the magnificent Gothic cathedrals of the Middle Ages, the artisans placed in the dark corners grotesque, demonic little carvings they called gargoyles. They were meant to be a reminder that there is no place where we can be entirely free of temptation. There is no church so holy, no home so sweet, no monastery so isolated, no convent so remote that temptation will not be found there. There's always danger, and so we must always be vigilant. We must keep watch and commit ourselves to the daily struggle against temptation.

This is why Our Lord in His infinite wisdom gave us the sacrament of His Mercy, the Sacrament of Penance! He gave it to us on that first Easter Sunday evening, when He appeared to the Apostles in the Upper Room after His Resurrection, a critical moment in the history of the Church. We are told about this in the Gospel of St. John: "He breathed on them, and said to them, 'Receive the Holy Spirit. If you forgive the sins of any, they are forgiven; if you retain the sins of any, they are retained'" (John 20:22–23).

Every Catholic should have those verses memorized. We should know them by heart so that we can be ready to answer whenever our faith is called into question on this matter. The Gospel shows us clearly that Jesus gave His disciples the power to forgive sins in His Name. But—and this is important—He did not give them the power to read minds! How could the disciples know which sins to forgive and which to retain if no one would confess? We have the practice of sacramental Confession because it has been handed down to us from the Apostles by the will of Our Lord and Savior Jesus Christ. That is why Confession, in one form or another, has been the practice of Christian believers from the very beginning.

Making a Holy Lent

What a sad thing it is that most Catholics today have forgotten what a great gift we have in the sacrament of Penance. When you leave the confessional after having made a really good, sincere Confession, it feels as if a physical burden has been lifted off your shoulders. You feel a real sense of relief. You feel so very close to Almighty God. I'm sure you've had that feeling—and if you haven't, give it a try!

You see, Jesus left us this sacrament because He knew well what sin and guilt can do to the human soul. They can tear the human soul apart—separate it from God. They can drive a person to despair. God knows we need to have some way to be free of sin and guilt because they can rob us of the inner peace and joy that should be ours as Christian believers—the peace and joy that come with having a clear conscience before God.

The human spirit needs to be at peace with God, and we need to be at peace with ourselves. We need to know for sure that God has forgiven us. We need to be able to experience God's merciful love as it touches our lives. There will be times in our lives, we know well, when we will need to make a new start spiritually, when we will need to wipe the slate clean and start over again. When we do this, we will need to be strengthened by God's grace to avoid the same sins in the future. That is how the sacrament of Confession helps to transform us interiorly.

The Sacrament of Confession

We can think of all kinds of ways to try to rationalize our sins away, all kinds of lame excuses not to go to Confession, even during Lent. How often do we hear Catholics say, "I don't need to go to Confession. After all, God understands me. He is going to forgive me no matter what. God is all loving. He is all merciful. He would never really punish me. God would never really condemn anyone! And everybody is doing the things that I do anyway!"

That is a very dangerous presumption. That is *the sin* of presumption — the idea that a person can live habitually in mortal sin and that God will turn a blind eye to it; the idea that God will not do exactly what He has revealed that He intends to do with those who die in the state of mortal sin. We must never gamble with our immortal souls this way. There is too much at stake.

Also, we too often hear these days remarks like this: "Why should I have to confess my sins to a priest? He's just a man like me. Why can't I just confess my sins directly to God?" The answer to that second question is, first, that it's good to confess your sins directly to God. There's nothing *wrong* with confessing your sins to God in private prayer; in fact, as part of a regular examination of conscience, this could be an excellent spiritual habit. But the fact is

Making a Holy Lent

that that is not the way that God established for our sins *to be forgiven!*

True faith is never a matter of doing your own thing. Rather, it is a matter of doing God's thing—worshipping God in the way that He wants to be worshipped, in the way He established in the Person of His Son. God's thing is Confession for the forgiveness of sins. It always has been and always will be, until the end of the age.

Remember that God has no need to be told what our sins are! God knows everything! What He is calling on us to do is penance—some kind of reparation for our sins against Him and against our neighbors. There is no penitential aspect to confessing your sins only in private prayer. God calls us to make reparation. That is why Jesus said, "Unless you repent you will all likewise perish" (Luke 13:3).

Let's face it: It can be a penance simply to have to go to Confession. It can be a very humbling experience, especially if you've been away for a long time. But your priest always understands that! Plus, the seal of the Confession is absolutely inviolable. Don't ever let foolish pride prevent you from taking advantage of God's offer of complete forgiveness—the healing, strengthening, transforming graces of the sacrament of Reconciliation. There's just about nothing more beautiful you can do than to make a good Confession during Lent.

The Sacrament of Confession

When you go to Confession, in addition to receiving the forgiveness of your sins through absolution, you also receive an outpouring of God's grace that will strengthen you from within. By the action of the Holy Spirit in your soul, that grace will help you to avoid mortal sin, to avoid occasions of sin, and to avoid forming willful attachments to sin. It will also help you to overcome temptation and to root out habitual faults in your spiritual life. Frequent Confession is a strong line of defense against sin, temptation, and the wiles of the devil.

When a Catholic stays away from Confession for a long time, what typically happens is that many of his sins will fade from his memory and never be confessed. And if he never makes an examination of conscience, his conscience will eventually grow desensitized to the seriousness of sin; he'll become more vulnerable to temptation, more than likely to fall into mortal sin in moments of weakness. That is why I recommend to everyone the practice of frequent Confession as our first line of defense against sin.

The beauty of the sacrament of Penance is that whenever you confess your sins to the best of your ability and the best of your memory—when you don't hold anything back and you are truly sorry and you have a firm purpose of amendment—you always leave the confessional with that confident assurance of God's complete forgiveness.

Making a Holy Lent

Many people worry unnecessarily about the sins they might have forgotten in their Confession. But the human mind is not like a computer that can access all the data it needs at just the right moment. Our memories are dimmed with our fallen human nature. When you've made a good Confession, all your sins are forgiven, so long as you have a contrite heart. God sees the interior of the heart. And if later you should remember some sin that you have forgotten to confess, just bring it up in your next Confession. It's as simple as that.

Some priests tell people not to come to Confession unless they have committed a mortal sin—and in the confessional they tell penitents who have not confessed any mortal sins not to come back again until they commit one! This is just bad spiritual theology. This is like a doctor telling a patient never to come in for a checkup until he is terminally ill. (Strictly speaking, we are obligated to confess only our mortal sins, but that is not to say that we cannot and should not confess even our venial sins—all the sins we can remember after having made a good examination of conscience—precisely because of those strengthening, healing graces.)

The idea is to avoid mortal sin completely and to seek true holiness of life! The objective is to become saints! Those who have lapsed into this complacent mind-set have forgotten about the power of sacramental grace — that it is an effective barrier against sins and a very effective means to personal holiness.

It is because of God's infinite love for us that He commands us to make use the sacrament of Penance. It is in this sacrament that we release the past to God's mercy, the present to His love, and the future to His providence.

Chapter 5

The Virtues of Charity and Chastity

The overriding theme of the season of Lent is repentance. When we talk about repentance, we must talk about the reality of personal sin. And when we talk about sin, we must talk about the Ten Commandments. And we should always talk about the Ten Commandments in the context of the virtue of charity — the true meaning of Christian love.

In the book of Exodus, there is a little postscript to the Ten Commandments — one more little "thou shalt not" that very few Christians are familiar with: "You shall not allege the example of the many as an excuse for doing wrong" (Exod. 23:2, NAB). Remember this, because

Making a Holy Lent

we'll be returning to this theme later: Christian morality is never about following the crowd, and Christian love is not about affirming what is popular or trendy.

When Jesus later reveals to us the two greatest commandments of the Divine Law, He shows us that *love* is the foundation of Christian virtue and living. Our Lord calls these the two greatest commandments because all of the Ten Commandments are summed up in them; we cannot consider them apart from one another: "You shall love the Lord your God with all your heart, and with all your soul, and with all your mind, and with all your strength.... You shall love your neighbor as yourself" (Mark 12:30–31). All the commandments fall somewhere within these two—love of God and love of neighbor.

The first three commandments govern our relationship with God, telling us our moral obligations toward God as Our Lord and Creator. The First Commandment tells us that we must worship God alone: "I am the LORD your God.... You shall have no other gods before me" (Exod. 20:2–3). No person or thing or idea or ambition can take first place in our hearts—the place that should rightfully belong to Almighty God. In other words, this commandment forbids idolatry.

Idolatry is not just some ancient sin practiced back in the days of the Old Testament by the Egyptians and the

Canaanites and the Babylonians. I can assure you that idolatry is alive and well among us today: It's just a different kind of idolatry.

But what exactly is idolatry? An idol is anything whatsoever that is worshipped in place of the True God. Anything that tends to crowd God out of your life can be an idol for you. The world today wants to do away with the worship of the True God and replace Him with the triune god money, sex, and power. These are the idols of modernity, and they are just as twisted and evil as Moloch or Baal. And I'm sorry to say that today it seems as if the false god has more worshippers than the True God does.

The Second Commandment, then, forbids us to take God's Holy Name in vain. This is generally only a venial sin—but take note that in the book of Exodus God says that He will personally remember those who use His Holy Name carelessly: "The LORD will not hold him guiltless" (Exod. 20:7).

The Third Commandment commands us to give God public worship on the Sabbath. For us in the New Covenant, that means going to Mass on Sundays and holy days of obligation, but it also means avoiding unnecessary servile work on the Sabbath. We should not treat Sunday just like any other day. It remains and always will be a day set apart for rest and worship, a day sacred to the Lord.

Making a Holy Lent

The other seven commandments cover our relations with our neighbors. They show us our moral obligation toward other people as fellow members of God's family. We don't need to list them all here to say this: All of these commandments are based on the foundation of love of God and, as a result, love of neighbor.

To love God is the greatest commandment because it is from God that we draw life itself; God is the reason for and the purpose of our lives on earth. And why did God create us? Well, that was one of the first questions in the old *Baltimore Catechism*. I once asked that question to an entire class of Catholic high school seniors, and not one could give me a correct answer. Here's the proper answer that was taught to and memorized by generations of Catholic students: "God made me to know Him, to love Him, and to serve Him in this world, and to be happy with Him for ever in heaven."[4]

No one can claim to love God if he does not love others and keep the Lord's commandments. We should therefore be especially careful to avoid sins against charity—against that sacred and divine bond of love that should exist between us and our neighbors. Sins against charity include

[4] *Baltimore Catechism* (1891), Lesson 1, question 6.

gossip, slander, detraction, rash judgment, insulting, reviling, or verbal or physical abuse of any kind.

One of the sins that we commit more often than we realize is detraction, which is unnecessarily revealing the hidden faults of others. Your neighbor's reputation is supposed to be held sacred in your sight: Every man and woman has a right to his or her good name. The Apostle James warned, "If any one thinks he is religious, and does not bridle his tongue but deceives his heart, this man's religion is vain" (James 1:26).

The Holy Scriptures tell us that if we don't love others, it is impossible to love God. The Apostle John wrote, "He who does not love does not know God; for God is love.... If any one says, 'I love God,' and hates his brother, he is a liar.... And this commandment we have from him, that he who loves God should love his brother also" (1 John 4:8, 20–21).

What does "love" actually mean? What does it mean to love in a truly Christian sense? The word "love" gets thrown around an awful lot these days, and many of us have lost sight of its true meaning. In fact, I think the word "love" has become one of the most misused and misunderstood words in the entire English language.

Making a Holy Lent

For example, we Americans say that we "love" all kinds of things. We love sports—boy, do we love sports! Sports has become an idol in the lives of many people today. If we were as enthusiastic about God in this country as we are about our favorite teams, this would be a nation of saints! We could convert the whole world!

We also love nice cars and nice clothes and shopping malls. We love hamburgers and cheeseburgers and french fries and pizza and ice cream. We love music and movies and television and computers and the stock market. We love too many things to mention. And then, of course, we love things that lead us even more directly away from God—money and sex and power.

Many think the Bible says that money is the root of all evil, but that's not quite right. The Apostle St. Paul actually says in his First Letter to Timothy that "the love of money is the root of all evils" (1 Tim. 6:10). And, of course, we know how people are in love with their wealth and their material possessions, their power, status, and worldly success.

Finally, some people love only themselves and their own selfish pleasures. And some people even love sin itself. That sounds extreme, but it's true—and it can happen to us more easily than you might think.

In the 1960s, everyone talked about "free love." What they really meant was "free sex," and the "love" they elevated was actually lust. Sex became just so much fun and games. And we are still reaping what we sowed more than two generations ago in the form of broken homes, broken marriages, broken families, broken hearts, and broken lives.

None of these things that I have mentioned here — the "love" of sports and consumerism and money and sex — has anything to do with Christian love. Christian love is a different kind of love: It is loving the way God loves.

I remember that even some Catholics participated in the confusion of the 1960s — not just by making sinful choices, but by *teaching* confusing half-truths about love and our Christian duties. In so doing, they planted seed of doubt in the minds of many Catholic young people. I should know: I was one of those confused Catholic young people!

I recall well that, within the Church, everyone was always talking about "love." It seemed as if every sermon we heard from the pulpit was about love. Every Sunday it was love, love, love, love, love! Of course, there's nothing wrong with that! But there must be clarity about what love *really* is — and the problem was that they never did tell us exactly what love is in a truly Christian sense. They would say that God loves us and that they loved us. Wonderful! But, it is sad but true to say, they didn't love us *enough* to tell us the *whole* truth. They told us only what they thought we wanted to hear.

They never told us, for example, that God's love makes moral demands on us. They never told us that love brings responsibilities to love God back and to honor His commandments. They never told us that true love sometimes demands sacrifice. They never told us that there are some sins that separate us from God's grace. They never told us, in other words, about the essential moral obligations that follow from Christian love.

Back then they always told us that God loves us unconditionally. And that's true! But then they implied (or sometimes said outright) that God was going to *accept* us unconditionally and that we didn't have to change in response to that loving call from God. We were led to believe that God doesn't care about what we do or how we live our lives. We were led to believe that our sins were not a big deal anymore — and we lived as if we believed it.

This may seem paradoxical to some, but I would suggest to you that the watering down of the Christian message is the reason most of the young Catholics I grew up with eventually left the Church. Watering down the Christian message is a surefire way to make a young person fall away from the Faith: Tell him that God doesn't care what he does. Tell him that God's going to accept him, no matter what. That'll do it every time. If the Church is just a social club for people to chitchat about a God who doesn't ask anything of us, well then, what's the point?

The truth is that God does loves us just the way we are — *but He loves us too much to let us stay that way.* God has created us to be saints. He is calling us to grow in holiness and virtue and wisdom and knowledge and understanding of our Faith. He is calling us to draw closer to Him at every moment, in everything that we do, every day of our lives.

Christian love, you see, is not an emotional or a sentimental kind of love. It is more than natural love; it is supernatural love! It transcends anything that we *feel* in our emotions or our bodies. If only we could get this message across to our young people, we could save many of them a lifetime of heartache.

For too many people, the practice of the spiritual life — whether in their own prayer life or in their relationships with others — is dependent upon a shallow, superficial, emotional high. All that will wear off. Christian love will not always give you an emotional uplift. In fact, at times it will bring the cross into your life. It will cause you to suffer.

Making a Holy Lent

Christian love is founded in the will. It is something we freely choose to put into practice because God commands us to love—even when it doesn't make us feel good and even when it involves suffering or personal sacrifice. It's like Jesus' unselfish and sacrificial love for us. It's a love that gives of itself for the good of others. It's loving others for the love of God.

This is the Christian virtue of charity, the greatest and the highest of all the virtues. Charity means loving God above all things; loving Him for His own sake; loving Him not for what He can do for you but for Who He is; loving Him because He is Love, Truth, Goodness, and Life itself. And as it relates to the love of neighbor, it means loving others for the love of God. It means loving your neighbor not because he deserves it but because God commands it. This is what St. Paul wrote about when he said:

> If I speak in the tongues of men and of angels, but have not love, I am a noisy gong or a clanging cymbal. And if I have prophetic powers, and understand all mysteries and all knowledge, and if I have all faith, so as to remove mountains, but have not love, I am nothing. If I give away all I have, and if I deliver my body to be burned, but have not love, I gain nothing. (1 Cor. 13:1–3)

The Virtues of Charity and Chastity

There are many ways to put Christian love into practice in our daily lives. For example, Christian love means loving your neighbor even when your neighbor isn't particularly lovable, even when your neighbor is hateful or miserable, knowing that God sometimes permits people like this to come into our lives to see whether we are willing to practice what we profess. Love means not withholding forgiveness, in spite of what you feel, so the healing process can begin. Love is trusting in God's grace. Love is the sacrifice you make to make a marriage work and to keep a family together in spite of all the pressures and hardships and temptations of modern living. Love can sometimes mean holding down a job that you hate for the sake of the people you love. Love is often the struggle to take care of sick or aging or disabled members of your family.

For married couples, love means recognizing the fact that, in the sight of Almighty God you don't have the right to stop loving your spouse! God intends that your covenant of love will last a lifetime — "till death do you part." Love is trying to live a life of Christian virtue and moral purity in a society in which sin is more popular than ever, in a culture that mocks Christian values. Love is trying to make time for prayer every day, even when time is short, knowing that prayer has the power to change your

Making a Holy Lent

life and the lives of others. Love is having the courage to tell someone who is close to you who is living a morally bad life that he or she is going the wrong way and needs to get right with God.

The greatest love of all for your neighbor is concern for his or her eternal salvation. The first of the spiritual works of mercy is to admonish the sinner. It is never mercy to affirm people in their sins or to turn a blind eye to wrong-doing. To love the sinner does not mean to love the sin as well. Jesus said, "For what will it profit a man, if he gains the whole world and forfeits his life?" (Matt. 16:26). This is what Christian love is all about.

Four times at the Last Supper Jesus said to the apostles some form of the following: "If you keep my command-ments, you will abide in my love.... This is my command-ment, that you love one another as I have loved you" (John 15:10, 12). The key phrase there is "as I have loved you." And how did Jesus love us? He loved us enough to suffer for us, to shed His Blood on the Cross for us, to die for us. That is why love finds its most perfect expression in the Cross of Jesus Christ, and why the Cross is the greatest symbol of love the world has ever known. We should think about this every time we look at a crucifix. Every time we receive Him in Holy Communion, we should think of that Precious Blood that He shed for us and that Sacred Heart that loved us so much and the terrible price that He paid for each one of us and for our redemption.

The Apostle John said, "He who says 'I know him' but disobeys his commandments is a liar, and the truth is not in him" (1 John 2:4). And Jesus told the Pharisees that "there is nothing outside a man which by going into him can defile him; but the things which come out of a man are what defile him" (Mark 7:15). The sins that emanate from within the human heart defile us. Our Lord named some of those evils: "evil thoughts, fornication, theft, murder, adultery, coveting, wickedness, deceit, licentiousness, envy, slander, pride, foolishness" (Mark 7:21–22). These are the things that can drive the Holy Spirit from the soul, resulting in a loss of Sanctifying Grace. These are the things that can cause the eternal loss of the soul — eternal separation from God in that state of eternal misery that Our Lord called Gehenna, or Hell.

Hell is real, and Hell is forever. Some people try to argue that Our Lord did not really mean all those things that He said about Hell in the Gospel. They say it was all just something Our Lord made up to frighten immature people into obedience. Don't ever be taken in by that kind of nonsense. No biblical figure spoke as much or as often

Making a Holy Lent

about the reality of Hell as did Our Lord Jesus Christ. He spoke about Hell twenty-eight times in the Gospels, and He made reference to eternal punishment about ninety times. We have to be aware of the very real possibility of eternal damnation. That is as much a part of God's revelation to us as anything else.

If there is no sin and if there is no Hell, then Our Lord suffered and died on Calvary for nothing! And this season of Lent has no meaning; the Stations of the Cross have no meaning; all the events of Holy Week have no meaning; all the events of Our Lord's Passion and death and Resurrection have no meaning! It was all in vain, all futile! But that cannot be.

There are many people today, including some Catholics, who think that everyone is going to be saved. They think that everybody is going to Heaven, no matter what they do, no matter what they believe, no matter how they live, no matter how they worship. Sure, maybe Hitler or Stalin or Jack the Ripper or Osama bin Laden won't quite make it, but everybody else is as good as in. They think that all you have to do to get to Heaven is to die. They think they can be saved without giving up their sins.

A great danger today is that we tend to focus almost exclusively on God's infinite love and infinite mercy at the expense of His infinite justice. Yes, God is all loving and all merciful, but He is also infinitely just. Those who will not respond to God's merciful love in this life will have to face God's justice in the life to come. That's God's Word to us.

Catholics in our country today are under tremendous, relentless social pressure to conform themselves to the pagan mores of contemporary culture. And millions are giving in. It seems as if every time I turn around, there is a new opinion poll saying that some distressingly high percentage of American Catholics disagree with Church teaching on this or that issue—abortion, contraception, sterilization, divorce and remarriage, euthanasia, self-abuse, homosexual acts, premarital sex. You name it, we'll disagree with it—even though these are some of the very same sins that are destroying the sanctity of marriage and human sexuality, destroying the sanctity of human life, destroying the sanctity of family life. They are the sins that are causing the very fabric of our society to unravel.

What should we make of these polls? What bearing should they have on what we believe? None whatsoever! In the entire Bible, there's only one account of a public opinion poll, and it was taken by Pontius Pilate on that first Good Friday. The consensus was to crucify Our Lord. The only scriptural opinion poll ended with the words, "Crucify Him! Away with Him!... We have no king but Caesar!" (John 19:15). You see, opinion polls might be

Making a Holy Lent

good in politics, but they're no good in religion. God's Word is eternal. God's Word is absolute.

God never left His Holy Word up for grabs. We are Catholics; we do not live by public opinion! We live by the Word of God. Right is still right when nobody's right, and wrong is still wrong when everybody's wrong. The truth is still the truth even when the truth is unpopular. That's why the Bible says, "Jesus Christ is the same yesterday and today and for ever" (Heb. 13:8).

We are living in very difficult times. It really takes heroic effort to put the Catholic Faith into practice today—especially for young people, because modern life presents them with more temptations against chastity, purity, and fortitude than you can imagine. All the means of social communication are being used to tempt them—movies and television and music and social media—and it's all supported by the deadliest form of seduction, peer pressure.

It's as if the world and the devil are constantly telling them, "Go for it! Forget about God. Don't listen to the Church. Don't listen to your parents. What do they know? They're backward and old-fashioned! You can have it all right now. Why should you have to wait? If it feels good, do it!" But God is telling you: Don't ruin your life. Don't hurt your family. Don't spoil your chances to have a happy, stable marriage and family life. And most of all, don't risk losing your place in Heaven by living in mortal sin.

History has proven time and time again that the rejection of the virtue of chastity and the Church's teaching on sexual morality leads inevitably to the destruction of the family. Next to the ruin of souls, the one thing Satan seeks most is the destruction of the family.

I had an old professor who used to compare the family to the atom. They are both the basic unit of their orders — the atom in the order of nature and the family in the order of society. But both also release terrible, uncontrollable forces when they are broken apart. With enough split atoms (and families), a chain reaction can destroy entire cities and nations.

Don't ever believe the lie that the Catholic Church teaches that human sexuality is evil or dirty. Exactly the opposite is true, because the Church teaches and has always taught that human sexuality, created by God and sanctioned by God, is not just good, but sacred. From the act of sexual union between a man and a woman, God brings human life into the world. Sex is the wellspring of life! The marital act involves the transmission of human life, and human life is sacred, made in the image and likeness of God.

Making a Holy Lent

Remember this: When God gives human life, He gives it forever. God brings every human soul into this world with an *eternal* destiny. Every human person God brings into the world is unique, precious, and unrepeatable. Every one possesses an intrinsic dignity and value, not because of what he or she can do or produce or consume, but because of who he or she is as a child of God.

That is why God designed human sexuality to be both life-giving *and* love-giving. These are the procreative and the unitive ends of marriage and sexuality, and they can never be morally separated from each other. This is why God ordained sex to take place only within the confines of a sacred covenant between one man and one woman before God—the sacrament of Marriage. And that is why every deliberate abuse of human sexuality—in thought or in action, committed alone or with another person—where there is full knowledge, sufficient reflection, and full consent of the will, is objectively gravely sinful. It breaks our relationship with God. That is how deadly serious God is about the sanctity of human life and the means by which He brings life into the world.

St. Paul taught the early Christians that the human body is never to be abused because it is a temple of the Holy Spirit. This is what he wrote in his First Letter to the Corinthians:

> Or do you not know that the unrighteous will not
> inherit the kingdom of God? Do not be deceived:
> neither the sexually immoral, nor idolaters, nor
> adulterers, nor men who practice homosexuality, nor
> thieves, nor the greedy, nor drunkards, nor revilers,
> nor swindlers will inherit the kingdom of God. And
> such were some of you. But you were washed, you
> were sanctified, you were justified in the name of
> the Lord Jesus Christ and by the Spirit of our God.
> (1 Cor. 6:9–11, ESV)

These are powerful words, and they might even seem harsh. But we must never forget that they were written under the inspiration of the Holy Spirit and that they apply to every people and every place and every time. God never asks the impossible of us! His mercy is greater than our sinfulness! There is no sin so great, no matter how terrible you might think it is, that God is not ready to forgive when we are willing to repent!

The spiritual life is a constant struggle, both every day and over the course of our lives, and we can't make it alone. Without the grace of God, it is impossible to escape the bondage of sinful habits. All of us feel the attractive power of sin in our lives, but the beautiful truth is that God makes available to all of us the grace we need to be

Making a Holy Lent

conformed to His Holy Will. When we trust in His mercy, when we turn to Him through the life of prayer, when we make time for God's inspired Word, and when we approach Him through the sacraments, especially through the sacrament of Penance, He will give us all the strength we need to endure and to thrive in this life.

So I am challenging you today to make a stand for Jesus Christ in your life. I am challenging you to swim against the shifting tides of public opinion. I am challenging you, especially young people, to reject the immoral lifestyles the world is offering today. I am challenging you to conform your life to God's wisdom and Will, even when His Will doesn't match your own desires and opinions, so that you can be a witness for Jesus Christ by your life of prayer, holiness, good works, and purity of heart. If you do this, the Holy Spirit will truly dwell in your soul each and every day of your life.

Chapter 6

The Danger of Pride and the Power of Humility

Let's begin this reflection on humility as the foundation of virtue with a reading from the letter of St. Paul to the Philippians:

> Though he was in the form of God, [Jesus] did not count equality with God a thing to be grasped, but emptied himself, taking the form of a servant, being born in the likeness of men. And being found in human form he humbled himself and became obedient unto death, even death on a cross. Therefore God has highly exalted him and bestowed on him the name which is above every name, that at the name of Jesus every knee should bow, in heaven and on

earth and under the earth, and every tongue confess that Jesus Christ is Lord, to the glory of God the Father. (Phil. 2:6–11)

Jesus is the model of perfect humility, and punishment for pride is built into the very order of God's creation. Jesus told us, "Whoever exalts himself will be humbled; whoever humbles himself will be exalted" (Matt. 23:12). It is essential to understand why pride is so dangerous to the life of the soul—why it has been considered the most dangerous of the seven capital sins.

Pride was the sin of Lucifer and the fallen angels, who said, "I will not serve." Pride was the sin of Adam and Eve, who wanted to be like God and to decide for themselves what is right and what is wrong, without reference to God. This pride resulted in disobedience and sin, thus bringing pain, suffering, sickness, and death into the world.

Pride is that exaggerated self-love that inclines us to see ourselves as superior to others. It is that insidious desire for self-exaltation that leads us to seek our own honor and glory apart from the honor and glory of God. Pride sees the self as the center of the universe, the measure of all truth, and the standard of all morality. Pride sets itself in opposition to God's wisdom and will and encourages one to see himself as the judge over God's Word and God's law.

The Danger of Pride and the Power of Humility

Pride will always seek to have its own way, to control, to dominate, and to manipulate.

When we examine our consciences and look back on our experience, invariably we see that many of our worst moments and bitter regrets can be traced back to our foolish pride. We all know it's true. Pride is the great destroyer of marriages, the stumbling block to holiness of life, the obstacle to grace and repentance, the mental block to forgiveness, peace, and reconciliation. It is the source of endless self-deception, vanity, and folly. Through it comes the lust for power; thus, it is the catalyst of anger, violence, and war. It is an affront to God, an open door to the devil, and the gateway to Hell. And if we let pride rule our lives, it will always be a disaster in the making, because, no matter how confident we might feel, it will always backfire on us in the end.

There's only one antidote for pride, and that's humility. The tendency to pride is overcome only by its corresponding virtue, humility, which is the root of all virtues. For all of us, there is a simple rule in the spiritual life: Where there is no humility, there can be no merit in your good works in the sight of Almighty God, and therefore there can be no sanctity. Pride, though it may be secret pride in the form of selfishness and ulterior motives, will cancel out the meritorious nature of your good works. In other words, you can't store up any treasure in Heaven if your treasure is tainted by pride.

So, what is humility? Here's a simple rule to keep in mind from St. Teresa of Avila: "Humility is truth." That is, humility is the moral virtue by which we have an accurate opinion of ourselves, seeing ourselves as God sees us. Humility is the virtue that restrains us in our unruly desire for personal glory and helps us to recognize the fact that there is an infinite distance between the creature and the Creator God, without Whom we are nothing and can do nothing. With Christ as our model, we can say that humility is the self-emptying that allows God to work in us with His grace.

The word "humility" comes from the Latin term *humus*, which means "earth," "soil," "dust," or "dirt." It reminds us of God's word to us in the book of Genesis: "You are dust, and to dust you shall return" (Gen. 3:19.) In the spiritual sense, this earthy etymology also reminds us that we are called to cultivate the garden of the soul so that it can bring forth good fruits — that is, good works and development of virtue. Anybody who has done any gardening knows well that you can't grow anything unless you have the right kind of soil. In the spiritual life, the good soil is always *humus* — humility. Humility reminds us that every good thing we have and every gift we enjoy come from God and not from within ourselves.

The Apostle St. Paul expresses this beautifully in his Second Letter to the Corinthians: "But we have this treasure in earthen vessels, to show that the transcendent power belongs to God and not to us" (2 Cor. 4:7). And St. Francis de Sales said, "Humility and charity are the principal virtues. They act as mother hens while all the other virtues follow them like little chicks."[5]

True humility should not be confused with timidity and mediocrity. True humility does not deny the gifts, talents, and abilities that God has given us. But it does mean that we don't claim those gifts *as our own*; rather, we recognize them as having come from God, knowing that He wants and expects and demands that we use those gifts to build up the Body of Christ, the Church, on earth for His greater honor and glory and for the salvation of souls.

In my years in the priesthood, I have known people who have a false conception of humility, people who will fall back on false humility as an excuse to do nothing — people

[5] St. Francis de Sales, *Letters*, fragment 17.

Making a Holy Lent

who have plenty of time and talent on their hands that they just don't use. When asked to get involved in some kind of apostolic work or ministry, they will say something like this: "Oh, Father, who am I? What can I do? I'll never amount to anything, little ol' me, good for nothing. I'd like to do more, but, you know, I'm so unworthy."

This is a very wrongheaded notion of what it means to serve God in humility. The key point is that the virtue of humility and trust in God go hand in hand. I think of a case of a brilliant, talented priest I knew who was tapped by the Vatican to become a bishop, but he declined, protesting that he was not worthy of the honor. And so another priest was selected—and fifteen years later, the diocese was in shambles and the bishop had resigned in scandal. Part of humility, therefore, is being open to God's plan for us.

Jesus told St. Paul, "My grace is sufficient for you, for my power is made perfect in weakness," which prompted the evangelist to write, "I will all the more gladly boast of my weaknesses, that the power of Christ may rest upon me" (2 Cor. 12:9). In another letter St. Paul said, "God chose what is low and despised in the world, even things that are not, to bring to nothing things that are, so that no human being might boast in the presence of God" (1 Cor. 1:28–29). St. Teresa of Avila is said to have remarked, "God plus one is an army." We are all little in the sight of

The Danger of Pride and the Power of Humility

Almighty God, and without Him we can do nothing. But thanks be to God, He is the One Who makes something out of nothing.

Now, we have to understand that to be a humble soul in God's sight does not mean that the Christian is called to be a doormat or a pushover in serious matters, especially when it comes to standing up for the truth and defending your faith and family. The saints were great in humility, but at the same time they were courageous, tenacious defenders of truth and opponents of evil.

The greatest obstacle to true Christian discipleship is pride; we have to struggle every day with the movements of pride within ourselves. The danger is that pride can be subtle and subconscious, so, if we are not constantly on our guard, the devil will use it to trip us up.

Why is pride so dangerous? Because we all want to be somebody. We all want to excel. We all want to stand out from the crowd. We all want the respect and admiration of others. In God's plan, however, there is only one way to excel and to succeed, and that is to be what God created us to be: saints. That's what it's all about.

We are all called to greatness in life, but we're called to be humble while we're called to be great. In fact, in the

Making a Holy Lent

sight of Heaven, humility is an essential part of greatness. Think of the life of our Blessed Mother Mary, the humblest of all of God's creatures, especially Her words in the Gospel of St. Luke:

> My soul magnifies the Lord,
> and my spirit rejoices in God my Savior,
> for he has regarded the low estate of his
>   handmaiden.
> For behold, henceforth all generations will call
>   me blessed;
> for he who is mighty has done great things for me,
> and holy is his name. (Luke 1:46–49)

Mary always acknowledged the great things God had done for Her. She didn't try to hide it, but rather always gave God the praise and the glory; she always directed everything back to God.

Greatness in God's eyes is not what greatness is in this sight of the world. We know all the things that the world holds in high esteem—wealth, success, status, power, pleasure, fame, physical beauty, athletic prowess—but all those things have no value whatsoever in the eternal view of Almighty God. What you truly are is what you are in the sight of the Lord—nothing more, nothing less. That is reality. Greatness in the sight of Heaven is the perfect fulfillment of God's Word and God's Will in your life. No matter how simple or hard it might be, greatness is found in following God's Will even the most ordinary circumstances of your daily life.

That is to say, greatness is holiness, and holiness is the alignment of the human will with the Will of Almighty God. That is how even the littlest, simplest, most hidden, humble soul can be great. And that's what makes a saint.

How can you discern the movements of pride within yourself? Here is a little diagnostic test for you:

- In your heart of hearts, do you see yourself as being better than others because of who you are, what you have, or what you know?
- In conversation with others, do you always seem to bring the subject back to yourself?
- Do you always seem to talk about yourself, your interests, and your affairs?
- Are you overly concerned about what people think of you?
- Are you always trying to make yourself look good in the sight of others?

Making a Holy Lent

- Are you always ready to stretch the truth—lie, that is—if that's what it takes to build yourself up?
- Do you always have to be right and hate to be contradicted?
- Do you hold on to your own opinions even when they are proven to be wrong?
- Do you find it easy to dissent from the teaching of the Church on faith and morals?
- Do you think that you know better than the Holy Spirit, the Holy Scriptures, the whole Church, and the whole company of the saints? (Bonus question: Are you ready to bet your immortal soul on that?)
- Are you ultrasensitive to criticism, and do you struggle to accept even mild fraternal correction?
- Do you find it easy to gossip?
- Do you take satisfaction in hearing somebody else being torn down?
- Do you jump on every chance to point out the faults and the mistakes of others?
- Do you find it hard to forgive even the slightest offense?
- Do you always feel a need to get even, and are always ready to hold a grudge?

- Do you organize your life for the sake of appearances, and do you always feel the need to be noticed?
- Do you perform your good works in order to win the praise of others, like the Pharisees who preferred the praise of men to the glory of God?

Does a lot of this sound familiar to you? Does it strike a nerve? These are the movements of pride.

The last question, then, is: How do we grow in the virtue of humility? The first thing to do always is simply to pray for it. The humble soul prays constantly out of radical dependence on God. The Bible says, "The prayer of the humble pierces the clouds, and he will not be consoled until it reaches the Lord" (Sir. 35:17). Second, remember that ordinarily God humbles us through humiliations, which come to us in big and small ways every day. We should accept these moments as permitted by God for our sanctification. Third, we should have a sense of humor — about ourselves most of all. Fourth, we should cultivate joyfulness in our lives. The humble soul is at peace in the hands of God. And finally, most important of all, we must imitate the One Who is the perfect model of humility, Jesus Christ, the Son of God; Jesus, Who said, "Blessed are the poor in spirit, for theirs is the kingdom of heaven" (Matt. 5:3); Jesus, Who humbled Himself to share in our humanity;

Making a Holy Lent

Jesus, Who taught His disciples to take the lowest place, who washed the feet of the Apostles, who came to serve and not to be served, and who said, "Take my yoke upon you, and learn from me; for I am gentle and lowly in heart" (Matt. 11:29).

Jesus Christ, the Eternal Word made Flesh, the Second Person of the Holy Trinity, the King of Kings and Lord of Lords, allowed Himself to be spat upon, abandoned, betrayed, denied, scourged, mocked, and crucified for love of us. For our salvation, He gave Himself up to a shameful public death. That, dear friend, is the humility of God.

Chapter 7

The Blessed Virgin Mary

In this final section of our Lenten mission, we will explore the special devotion that every Christian should have for the Mother of Our Savior. It was by the Will of God that Our Lord and Savior Jesus Christ became Man and came into this world through the faithful, humble, sinless Virgin Mary.

The greatest event in the history of the world—the Incarnation—took place in Mary's virginal womb. Mary is truly the Mother of God. To deny that Mary is the Mother of God is implicitly to deny the divinity of Christ, and that is to deny the very essence of what it means to be Christian. Mary is the Mother specially chosen, prepared, and formed by God to be His! Her mission, given to her by God, is to bring Jesus Christ into our world and into our lives, leading us always closer to Her Son.

Making a Holy Lent

Just as it was and is the Will of God that Jesus should come to us through Mary, so it is also God's Will that we should come to Jesus in the most intimate way through His Mother! That is why, through the centuries, the great saints of the Church have practiced devotion to Our Lady as a way to give special honor to Christ. The saints knew that Mary always reflects the Light of Christ: Her "soul magnifies the Lord" (Luke 1:46). The saints knew that true devotion to Mary always leads to where the Light of Christ shines most brightly upon earth—that is, to the Holy Eucharist!

Let us consider the place of Our Blessed Mother in salvation history. Mary is the first Christian and the supreme witness to the events of the Gospel. She participated in the events of Our Lord's entire life in a way that no one else could have, especially during the thirty years of Our Lord's hidden life at Nazareth. From the stable in Bethlehem to the foot of the Cross at Cavalry, no one ever knew or loved the Son of God as His Holy Mother, Mary, did.

Archbishop Sheen used to say that, in the mind of Almighty God, there are two visions of each one of us—one as we are, and one as He wants us to be. The objective in the spiritual life is to bring those two images into accord—to transform, through His grace, *what we are* into what God *wants us to be*. In all of time, there has been only one human person for whom God has had only one image: the Blessed Virgin Mary. She fulfilled the dream. She achieved the perfect fulfillment of God's Word and God's Will in Her life. That is why She is always a model of virtue and holiness for us to imitate.

I have a friend who became a Catholic about fifteen years ago. When he finally came into the Church, he did so with a tremendous zeal for the Faith, as converts so often do. But the one thing he found hardest to understand about Catholics was our devotion to Mary. He had always been told that there is nothing in Sacred Scripture that would lead anyone to have a special devotion to the Blessed Mother.

But then one day he sat down with his Bible, and before he started to read, he did what everyone should do before reading the Sacred Scriptures: He said a prayer to the Holy Spirit, the Spirit of Truth, to open his mind and his heart to God's revelation. Then he opened his Bible at random, and right away his eyes fixed on the first chapter of the Gospel of Luke, to the section about Mary's trip to visit with St. Elizabeth. And he read those words spoken by St. Elizabeth, the mother of St. John the Baptist: "Blessed are you among women, and blessed is the fruit of your womb! And why is this granted me, that the mother of my Lord should come to me?" (Luke 1:42–43).

And then he kept reading in the same chapter until he came upon Our Lady's own words: "All generations will call me blessed" (Luke 1:48). After he had a chance to meditate on all those words for a short time, what seemed so hard to understand before suddenly became so clear and obvious to him, and he wondered how he could ever have overlooked those verses for so many years! And today that same man has a powerful devotion to the Mother of Our Savior.

Now, it is important that Catholics understand that we don't *worship* Mary! Mary is not God; She is a created being just as we are. Mary is, however, the masterpiece of God's creation—the masterpiece of His grace on earth and His glory in Heaven. God is the Divine Artist, and a great artist is never offended when his masterpiece is admired and honored. So, no, we don't worship Mary; we honor her.

We honor Mary, quite simply, because Her Son honored Her! The Fourth Commandment tells us to "honor thy Father and thy Mother." And we know that the One who kept the Ten Commandments most perfectly was Jesus Christ Himself. In so doing, He left us an example to follow in all parts of our lives. Jesus would have given His Holy Mother the most perfect honor a son could ever give, and Scripture tells us that we are to imitate Christ in all things (see 1 Cor. 11:1). The essence of the spiritual life is the imitation of Christ. So, when we honor Mary, we are imitating Christ!

Mary is a unique woman chosen for a unique mission: She was the one Mother Whose Child came into this world not to live, but to die. Jesus Christ, the Son of God and the Son of Mary, came *in order to* die for us on the Cross, to redeem us from sin. He came into this world to be the image of the invisible God—all loving and all sacrificing. He came to show us the way to Heaven and to the Father, and He came to establish a New and Everlasting Covenant, a covenant that He sealed in His Blood!

The word "covenant" is very important in our Faith, so much so that Our Lord used it only once in the Gospel—at one of the most solemn moments of His life, the Last Supper: "This is my blood of the covenant, which is poured out for many" (Mark 14:24).

A covenant is by definition a sacred family bond; it is a blood bond; it is a bond that can never be broken once it has been sealed and ratified. Jesus founded the Catholic Church to be God's *covenant* family on earth. So we say rightly that the Church is a true family. All Christians are

Making a Holy Lent

adopted sons and daughters of God through Jesus Christ by virtue of our Baptism, and that makes us true brothers and sisters in God's covenant family.

But do you think that God would leave His spiritual family without a Mother? What is a family without a mother's love, a mother's care, a mother's help and prayers? No family is ever complete without a mother. A mother is the heart of a family; she is a source of love and consolation and refuge in times of trouble. A mother's love is one of the most powerful forms of human love in all of creation!

Doesn't it make sense that God, Whose love is constantly searching for more and more of our love, in return for His infinite love, would appeal to our hearts through one of the most powerful forms of love in His creation — a mother's love? Doesn't it make sense that the Sacred Heart of Jesus would appeal to our human hearts through the Immaculate Heart of Mary? God, in His infinite wisdom, gave His spiritual family the most loving Mother of all.

The Gospels tell us quite a lot about Mary and about Her relationship with God, Her incomparable virtue, and Her sublime holiness of life, beginning at the time when She was a young woman, probably just a teenager, living in Nazareth and betrothed to a man named Joseph. You can imagine all the plans that Mary must have had at that time—all the things She had to look forward to and the kind of life She must have expected. But all of that was changed in a single instant when God sent the Archangel Gabriel to call Her to be the Virgin Mother of the Redeemer.

When St. Gabriel came to call Our Lady, he spoke to Her with words that no angel had ever addressed to a human being before: "Hail, full of grace!" (Luke 1:28). That was a Heavenly salute—an angelic salutation! Those were words of honor and praise to Mary, the lowly handmaid of the Lord—Mary, full of grace before Our Lord's Birth, full of grace without Baptism. What better evidence could we need for the truth of the Immaculate Conception than the words of the archangel who stands before God's throne? No Christian should ever be ashamed or afraid to give Mary the honor that She deserves, the honor that is rightly due to Her as the Virgin Mother of God's only-begotten Son!

And when God called Mary, She answered His call. Without any hesitations or reservations or doubts or excuses, She said yes to God with absolute faith and trust in His Word: "Behold, I am the handmaid of the Lord; let it be to me according to your word" (Luke 1:38). With those words She made one of the most perfect acts of faith in

Making a Holy Lent

all of salvation history. Mary surrendered Her life — Her body, Her heart, Her soul, all Her hopes and plans for the future — completely to God. She loved God so much that in that one instant, She gave everything She had to give so that God's Will could be done in Her, so that God's plan for our salvation could be carried out, so that Jesus could be the center and the purpose of Her life. And She let the Holy Spirit lead Her and guide Her perfectly at every moment. In the Virginal Conception of Her Divine Son, Mary became the Spouse of the Holy Spirit.

Therefore, we can say that in the spiritual life, there is a very simple formula: The Holy Spirit plus Mary brings forth Jesus Christ! All through Mary's life there was no limit to Her faith, hope, and love, no end to Her goodness, generosity, and humility. Mary abandoned Herself totally to God's providence, knowing that God makes all things work together for the good of those who love Him (see Rom. 8:28), knowing that God can arrange things for our happiness far, far better that we ever can for ourselves — if only we accept His holy Will and follow His loving plan for our lives, come what may! No human person ever loved God as much as Mary did.

That is why, for Catholics, the Virgin Mary has always been the perfect example of a life totally dedicated to God, a model of virtue and holiness to imitate! That is why She was the one specially chosen by God, before time began, and preserved free from every stain of sin. From the very first moment of Her existence, by a singular divine privilege given by God to Her alone, the merits of Our Lord's Passion and death on the Cross were all applied in advance to her magnificent, resplendent soul. She is the one full of grace. She is the Immaculate Conception, free from all sin and thus free to concentrate all the powers of Her being toward the fulfillment of God's plan for our redemption.

In the book of Revelation, Mary appears for the last time in Scripture. But this time the humble handmaid of the Lord is "the Woman clothed with the sun," "the Queen of Heaven."

> Then God's temple in heaven was opened, and the ark of his covenant was seen within his temple.... And a great portent appeared in heaven, a woman clothed with the sun, with the moon under her feet, and on her head a crown of twelve stars.... She brought forth a male child, one who is to rule all the nations with a rod of iron. (Rev. 11:19; 12:1, 5)

In the Old Testament, God commanded the Israelites to build the Ark of the Covenant, inside of which they

Making a Holy Lent

placed the two stone tablets on which God had written the Ten Commandments—the same stones Moses had carried down from Mount Sinai. The Ark of the Covenant carried and contained God's Written Word and Law. But in Revelation, Mary is the new Ark of the New Covenant because She carried Jesus Christ, God's Eternal and Living Word in Her virginal womb.

And She wears that crown of twelve stars because She is a true Queen! Mary is the Queen of Heaven, the Queen of the Apostles, the Queen and Mother of the Church, the Queen and Mother of all Christians everywhere, higher than angels and men. Mary is a Queen because Jesus is a King.

Why, then, is the moon also a symbol for Mary? The moon gives no light of its own; rather, it reflects the light of the sun. This is exactly what Mary does: She is not the Light, but in her humility She reflects the Light to us. She is the perfect reflection of Her Divine Son, Jesus Christ, Who is the True Light of the World.

By Her glorious Assumption, the Blessed Virgin Mary has been taken up body and soul to be with Her Son forever in Heaven. And so She is in a unique, privileged position to be able to help us through Her prayers.

This is key to understanding Catholic devotion to Mary. On Calvary, Mary stood at the foot of the Cross and watched Her only Son die a most horrible death. She suffered there a worse pain than any mother could ever endure. She made the greatest sacrifice God could ever call upon a mother to make. And then Our Lord, hanging in agony on the Cross, looked down upon Mary and upon St. John, the beloved disciple, and He said to St. John, "Behold, your Mother!" (John 19:27).

With these dying words, Our Lord gave one of His greatest gifts to us: His own loving Mother to be a spiritual Mother to us all. The Gospel says, "And from that hour the disciple [John] took her to his own home" (John 19:27). He took Mary to be his own Mother. Is that what we do? Do we take Mary into our homes? Do we take Her to be our spiritual Mother? Do we take Her to be our Queen, our Patroness, our Intercessor with Her Divine Son? Nothing can be more pleasing to Our Lord than when we do these things in humility and thanksgiving for the gift He has given us.

In no way does our devotion to Mary detract from the honor and glory that should be given to Christ alone! That is foolishness! All the praises given to Mary do nothing but glorify God, Who made Her who She is. Mary is in no conceivable way an obstacle blocking the way to Heaven or to Jesus! She *leads* the way; She *clears* the way; She *lights* the way; She *guides* us on the way to Her Son. That is why we love Mary and honor Her the way we do!

Making a Holy Lent

Our Blessed Mother has appeared in our world numerous times since her Assumption—in Lourdes and Knock, Fatima and Akita. Why does she do this? Mary never ceases to be our Most loving Mother: When a mother rushes to her children, it is because she knows they are in danger. And so we need to recognize that the world is in danger; the Church is in danger; families are in danger; souls are in danger. Our Lady is calling upon all of us to become a great force of prayer and reparation in the world.

By the grace of God, Mary has given us a wonderful and powerful weapon to fight with in the spiritual battle of our time: the Holy Rosary. St. Padre Pio, the great mystic of the last century who bore the marks of Christ's wounds, prayed the Rosary constantly, calling it his shield against Satan. He had a simple motto, "Pray, hope, and don't worry." But the Rosary is also an instrument of God's mercy—a way to bring about the conversion of sinners, peace in our homes, peace in our families, and peace in our hearts. The Rosary is a lifeline that God holds out to His people today and every day.

We all have to ask ourselves: How important to us is the Faith and salvation of our family? Is it important enough to come together for the fifteen or twenty minutes a day it takes to pray the family Rosary, thereby answering a request directly from Heaven? Almighty God will grant many special graces to those families who come together to pray the Rosary. Is there some special person you need to pray for? Is there some conversion you're asking Almighty God to grant to you? Is there some special intention you have, some grace you need? Is there some sin you struggle with, some temptation you have to overcome? We all can answers yes to most, if not all, of these questions, and so why not ask for the help of Our Lady?

The Blessed Virgin Mary wants to keep all of us within the secure refuge of Her Immaculate Heart. She wants to lead us and guide us and protect us through the dangerous and difficult days to come. No one who has trusted in Her has ever been disappointed.

Fr. William Casey, C.P.M.

Father Casey is a native of Philadelphia, Pennsylvania, and a 1979 graduate of Temple University. After graduating from college, he served as an officer in the U.S. Army. Upon leaving the Army, he entered the Congregation of the Fathers of Mercy. He studied philosophy at Christendom College and theology at Holy Apostles Seminary and was ordained to the priesthood in 1991. From 1997 to 2009, Fr. Casey served as the Superior General of the Congregation. Father attributes his call to the priesthood to the Mercy of God, his love for the study of Sacred Scripture, and his strong devotion to the Sacred Heart of Jesus and the Immaculate Heart of Mary.